A Gourmand in Training is a work of nonfiction based on my recollection of events and life experiences. Some of the names of the individuals included in this book have been changed in order to protect their identities and to respect their privacy.

2013 Carpe Diem Consulting Inc.
Copyright ©2013 by Eric Arrouzé

Published In Canada by Carpe Diem Consulting Inc. in Vancouver, British Columbia.

I would like to thank everyone who contributed to this book, starting with my family and the people around me who play colorful roles in each story.

A special thank you to my wife Frédérique, who has encouraged and supported me in all my projects. As my web designer, photographer and advisor, she has also been an active contributor to my success.

On the more technical side, I want to acknowledge the work of my team: Cory for the book design, Gladis for translating all my French into readable English, and last but not least, my "feedback committee": Brenda, Gwen, Isabelle, Michelle and Peter. I feel privileged to have worked with you all, and I hope that the end result has made you proud. I am looking forward to working with you again on the next book.

Contents

III

CONTENTS

PREFACE

While some people are good at painting, playing an instrument or singing, I have been told more than once that I am good at storytelling. As a chef instructor, I teach people how to cook, yet somehow, a certain dish or an ingredient always triggers a story. My stories are sometimes educational, but always fun, entertaining or touching. Over the years, my students have remarked time and again that I should write a book to share these stories with a wider audience.

The irony of it is that one day at school my childhood English teacher told me that I would never be able to speak English. Although my mastery of the language is still not perfect, and my strong accent definitely betrays my European origin, I sometimes wonder how she would react knowing that I was now living in an English speaking country and making a living teaching in a language that, according to her, I was never supposed to know. Luckily, her remark did not stop me from embarking on life-changing experiences; perhaps her rigid stance actually challenged me to prove her wrong.

My story shows that everything is possible for those who want it enough. Anyone can achieve anything they want; the key is to do it one step at a time. Personally, I never put limits on my career or things I want to do. Sometimes the path is hard, but I keep going, and steps turn into milestones.

I was born and raised in a small town in French Pyrénées, near the Spanish border. I am the youngest of a family of four siblings, and while growing up we lived on the salary of my dad, who was a mason. Early on, I discovered my passion for food thanks to my grandmother Mamie Augusta. Shortly after, I discovered my other passion: travel. Being a cook (you have to earn the title of chef with experience), I was able to travel all over Europe, climbing the hierarchy of the kitchen, absorbing knowledge, honing my skills, earning my grade in the kitchen as head chef, one step at a time. When I finally became head chef in a luxury hotel on the French Riviera at age twenty-three, managing a team of fourteen, I thought I had it all, but it turned out that I was soon ready for a new challenge.

I cannot say that Canada has always been a dream, but somehow, I arrived in Montreal in 1993. I did not know anybody, and had never been there before. After two and a half years (including three winters), I moved to Vancouver and worked as a chef before joining a private school in Vancouver to become Chef Instructor. I worked there for three years. That is where I discovered my third passion: Teaching. Sharing my knowledge and teaching people how to cook professionally was so rewarding; it was a new beginning. But after a while it was time to move on. I wanted to teach in the public system, but I had no diploma and realized that I was missing some education, so I went back to school to get my BC Provincial Instructor Diploma to become a better instructor. I worked at Vancouver Community College for about a year and a half, before losing my job in 2001 because of budget cuts by the provincial government.

Unemployed, I was eligible for the Self Employment Program, a year long professional business development program, that helped me start my current company. My goal was to create a business where I could do what I love: cooking and teaching. That is what I have been doing since then. I offer private cooking classes and cooking parties to individuals as well as team building cooking classes. I have also been teaching culinary arts at UBC Continuing Studies for more than 10 years. In 2006, I began creating and leading culinary travel programs to Europe and Canada. Do you see how I found a way to combine my three passions?

V

There is nothing I enjoy more than when one of my students tells me how I contributed to his or her life. It makes me realize that everything that happens, every person that you meet, plays a role in who you are and what you do as long as you maintain true to your vision.

Although my story is not finished, by sharing some episodes, I want to make you laugh, make you think, inspire you, make you hungry and, above all, make you feel good. I hope that you will enjoy the stories of this first book in my series.

To my loving Grandmother, Mamie Augusta

Cooking is like love. It should be entered into with abandon or not at all.

-Harriet Van Horne
Vogue Magazine 1956

ONE

Mamie Makes
King Henry IV's Garbure

With the sleeve of my jacket, I wipe the condensation off the window of
the school bus that takes me downtown. It is 1976, I am nine years old
and about to make a discovery that will change my life forever.

Just like every other Wednesday, I am on my way to my grandmother's. She lives
in the old neighborhood around Château de Pau, also known as Pau Castle. The
château is forever linked to King Henry IV who was born in Pau (but not in the
castle) in 1553. This imposing structure not only dominates the central portion of
the city; it also casts its royal shadow over my humble existence. I live on the other
side of the city, in the suburb of Ousse des bois, which is quite a romantic name for
a place filled with rows of cement-colored buildings.

Ousse des bois was created as part of a post-World War II construction project
to allow people with modest incomes to find decent housing. It was idyllic — in
theory only. In truth it was a rough, urban place that had dozens of four-story
rectangular buildings, with 120 apartments in each, and a handful of twenty-story
towers. To this day, locals refer to these dwellings as "rabbit hutches." Authorities
have another name: LCH, or low-cost housing. It is a blue-collar neighborhood
where residents are immigrants, gang members and belong to families who barely

make ends meet. It is said to be a "hot," or troubled neighborhood, well-known by the government as one of the toughest suburbs in France.

I live with my family at the end of the bus line. The location made it seem like we have reached a dead-end in life, where no exit is possible. The only way to leave is to take the bus in the opposite direction. But to where? For most residents — nowhere: their school, their work, their entire life was Ousse des bois. They don't know any place else.

But when my family and I hop on the city bus, we know where we are going. To Mamie's! Her small apartment is our garden, our paradise, our escape. That is why leaving our listless neighborhood delighted me.

On this particular Wednesday, it is early afternoon when I arrive alone at 9 Parlement Street, the entrance to Mamie's apartment building. As I climb the stairs to the top floor, the old winding staircase creaks beneath my feet. It is a 17th-Century building and although it has water and electricity, the vestiges of the most recent renovations seem to date back to the 1800s.

I am impatient to get to the apartment to discover what Mamie is lovingly preparing for us for dinner tonight. As I push open the wooden door, I see that Mamie is already busy in the kitchen preparing a garbure Béarnaise, a hearty peasant-style soup.

"Here you are. I was waiting for you," Mamie greets me. "Take a seat on the stool and watch."

Mamie's place isn't lavish, but the small three-room apartment seems to suit her. An organized and cheery mess prevails in the kitchen. Vegetables on the table, the cutting board ready for use, and Mamie standing in front of it, her favorite knife in hand. She puts on quite a show. She grabs an onion and says, "Eric, are you ready? Watch. We are going to start with the onions. Pay attention, because one day you will be the one preparing the garbure for me!"

Me? I think. Cooking for you, Mamie? Impossible!

I was a boy. I didn't dare think about such things. It had never really dawned on me that one day I too might have impressive skills. Yet, despite my doubts, something clicked in my brain. At least I think it did. Because thinking back on that moment, I believe it was the beginning of my long journey — my quest — to become a chef.

2

I loved to watch Mamie. The way she handled the vegetables and other ingredients was so inviting. Sometimes I wanted so badly to grab the knife to help her.

But I don't have permission to touch what she calls her "tools." It will take time for me to earn that right. That is why on this day, I am still convinced that I will never cook as well as Mamie.

So I prop myself up on the stool and observe her every move. She cuts the vegetables with dexterity and speed. With a big, slightly rusted metal knife, she peels and cuts the onions while holding a slice of dry bread in the corner of her mouth. She explains that biting the bread prevents her from crying as it absorbs the strong essence by the onions.

I am spellbound by her knowledge!

A tear swells in the corner of her eye and furtively rolls down her cheek, which resembles one of those textured relief maps of France seen in tourist shops. Her facial complexion is pocked with so many highways, crossroads and detours that the tear will probably never reach her chin — it will evaporate first!

"Mamie! Are you crying?" I laugh.

"Of course not, my boy."

"But, Mamie, I see a tear. So you are still sensitive … sniff… to onions?" As I tease her, I don't want to admit that my nose is starting to itch.

"Eric, it isn't the onions; it's cigarette smoke that blew into my eyes."

I forgot to mention, Mamie smokes Marlboro cigarettes.

Picture this: an elderly woman holds a large onion in her left hand while cutting the root side with the knife she wields in her right hand. A piece of bread sticks out the left side of her mouth, while in the opposite corner a smoldering Marlboro dangles from her lips. That's Mamie.

"Ha, ha, ha!"

"Why are you laughing, child?"

I can't stop myself because I see that the onions have indeed made my Mamie's eyes itch.

I like to kid Mamie, but while I laugh, I cry and sniffle, too.

The onions are cut, thrown into a large black cast-iron cooking pot where a big spoonful of duck fat is slowly melting. Now it is time for the carrots and the turnips. They are washed in cold water. Mamie's fingers slide rapidly, casually but also carefully across the vegetable skins to remove all traces of soil and sand. There is a combination of roughness and tenderness in Mamie's gestures. As I watch, the onions are making a joyous sizzling sound in the pot and this faint noise adds to the merry mood in the kitchen.

The vegetable dance continues. Now the leeks meet the knife. A fast cut removes their white beards. Their bodies are chopped into four pieces and go under the tap for a complete wash. Under the spray of cold water, they look like disjointed scarecrows after a good rain. It makes me laugh. Here are the gentlemen leeks, closely shaved and bathed, no longer coated in remnants of mud. Soon, they will revisit Mamie's relentless knife. But for now, they are a heap of even pieces, in shades of green that range from pale, almost white, to deep emerald. A beautiful sight!

And then wham !

With a skilled flick of the wrist, a steady and swift hand, the chopped leeks join the onions. Mamie pushes the cooking pot onto the warmest part of the wood stove and mixes the vegetables briskly to make them sweat fully. I am also heating up in this small kitchen, as though I am melting with the onions and steaming with the leeks. Or maybe it is merely my heart warming to the heavenly scent — finer than any French perfume — that the vegetables release as they surrender to Mamie's will. The song of sizzle and steam is soft and pleasant and makes me drowsy.
Mamie continues her loving tutorial, telling me about the importance of browning the leeks and other vegetables well to make them tender and amplify their aromas.

"But make sure they don't burn, Eric."
"Why?"
"That would change their taste, and not for the better."

I listen to every word while keeping my eyes on Mamie's hands. It is an unbelievable show of skill. Constantly moving, she turns to the right, to the left, takes a vegetable, peels and cuts it into thin slices, and then stirs the pot once with a

CHAPTER ONE

wooden spoon. She is multi-tasking without effort, without stopping to think; all the while explaining in detail the what and why of her actions.

She shows me the handsome vegetables she bought in a special area of the market, yet complains about prices. The market is a covered area close to Les Halles, Pau's permanent marketplace, where local farmers can sell their produce.

"But Mamie, if produce is so expensive why don't you go someplace else, to a store?" I ask her.

"Ah! That's out of the question. The vegetables may be more expensive, but we know where they are from and how they grew."

"So."

"So? Vegetables from the store, most of the time, are grown in greenhouses that resemble factories made of plastic and glass. The vegetables are hosed down and it looks like they are sun tanning under giant light bulbs. They never had the good country air, rain water and sun, nor did they ever have the care of the farmer who knows when they are ready to harvest. Ripe food is good to eat, yes?"

Mamie is teaching me that good food is a living, breathing part of life. We must care for our food as we care for each other, or it won't sustain us.

She goes on, "The vegetables in the stores, in order to be shelved longer, are picked before they have the time to ripen — and that doesn't take into account the chemical products which helped them grow faster."
Chemicals? I think. In food? Not in Mamie's kitchen!

As the aromas fill the air, Grandmother tells me about the people she encounters at the market; it's a long list and she has much to say. It's entertaining, but ...

The truth is, Mamie is considered a "character" in the city of Pau. She is everyone's Mamie, especially in her own neighborhood. Often, the corner pizzeria delivers a free pizza to her, or the baker brings her pastries. In exchange, Mamie gives them fish she catches in the local Gave de Pau river.

A character, yes, and a generous and beloved one.

TWO

Mamie & Pierre

Mamie Augusta was born in 1905 in Aramits, a small Bearnese village, where she spent her childhood and lived through World War I. The thirteenth of fourteen children in the Lamothes family, she was married at twenty to Pierre Arrouzé, a man from the village of Momas, whom she met in a dance hall.

Mamie and Pierre had three children. The first, Batiste, arrived after two years of marriage, but died from tuberculosis at the age of one. That caused my grandmother much grief throughout her life and every time we went to Momas, we would always stop by the cemetery located at the village entrance.

Seven years later, she gave birth to my father, Jean, and four years after that, on the eve of the World War II, my Aunt Liliane was born.

Grandfather Pierre, whom I never met because he passed away from tuberculosis in 1942, was a mesmerizing and charismatic man, according to Mamie, who referred to him as her soul mate. He was good looking and well versed. He spoke seven languages fluently and traveled throughout the world, thanks to his job as a maître d'hôtel on the most luxurious ship of his era.

The Normandy was the fastest ship in the world when she left the Saint-Nazaire shipyard in 1932. She could make the transatlantic commute between the French port of Le Havre and New York in five days at a speed of thirty knots. Regarded by many to be the most beautiful ship ever built, the Normandy was also the world's largest ocean liner. No palace on earth could equal the luxury and comfort of this floating dream vessel.

And nothing was more spectacular than the first-class dining room. Running ninety-three meters in length, it was almost as long as a football field, two stories high and could seat seven hundred diners. Passengers entered through twenty-foot high bronze-covered doors, illuminated by tall columns of Lalique glass.

At sixty meters long, the kitchen was equally impressive. It accommodated seventy-six chefs and a hundred waiters who served more than four thousand meals per day. The cuisine was the most refined of that era and guests were served on the finest Limoges porcelain. An army of liveried waiters, led by a handful of maître d', including my grandfather, served meals in the continental fashion on very big, heavy, silver dishes. The best French wines were poured into lavish Baccarat crystal glasses. All the dishes were unique in keeping with the ship's image.

In 1940, after only four years of service, the Normandy was seized by the American Navy in New York harbor, and plans were made to convert her into a troop ship for more than 10,000 soldiers. Two years later, before the conversion could be completed, the ship caught fire and capsized under the weight of the water discharged by firefighters.

But Grandfather Pierre left the high seas before the Normandy was requisitioned and became a maître d' in another luxurious place — Le Casino de La Jetée Promenade and its restaurant La Véranda located in a palace in Nice, the beautiful Mediterranean city on France's southeastern coast.

The casino, which enjoyed a rebirth at the beginning of the 20th century, was originally built on stilts along the Nice beach next to the famous Promenade des Anglais, a walkway constructed by the British in the late 18th century. Unfortunately, the bell tolled for both the casino and this majestic structure of glass and steel with the arrival of German occupation troops on November 12, 1942.

The casino was forced to close its doors on December 20, 1942, and

7

in January 1944, the Germans ordered the demolition of the magnificent Promenade. They were hungry for its resources, the one thousand tons of copper and four thousand tons of steel used to build the jetty.

My grandfather never witnessed these events. Sick and weak, Pierre returned to Béarn, where he died in 1942.

Mamie would speak of this worldly man as someone who cherished her, and made her shiver with just one kiss on her neck. That was the legend of Pierre. But there was another side to my grandfather.

This refined and educated man who made grandmother so happy had a vice: gambling. An incorrigible and incessant roulette and baccarat player, he won and lost enormous sums, which made Mamie miserable. Once he even had to settle his debt in a gun duel. My grandfather had honour, I'll give him that. I never did learn the whole story, and, frankly, I really didn't want to know: a mix of reality and legend was good enough for me.

Back to the Garbure

As she makes the garbure, Mamie talks to me about the people she saw on her trip to the market. She names individuals I don't know so I listen to her absent-mindedly, until she mentions having seen my Uncle Jean and Aunt Jeannette, both of whom who are actually Dad's cousins, but we love them as uncle and aunt. They had come to sell their chickens, eggs and rabbits. Jean was a blacksmith and owner of a farm in Momas, 30 kilometers north of Pau. I enjoyed my family's occasional Sunday visits there. I had so much fun on the farm with my cousin Dédé, chasing the turkeys and feeding the pigs.

Once more I ask Mamie to take me to the market. Up to now, she has always refused on the grounds that it is too crowded, I am too small and I would get lost, as I am a restless child.

So I am very surprised when she tells me that she will take me there soon, early in the morning at 9 a.m. to avoid the rush. I am so excited I can hardly wait! I am convinced that if so many people go to the market, it must be a very special place. But Mamie has one condition:

"You will have to spend the night here."

"Friday night?"

"Yes, my dear."

I barely contain my excitement. "Oh, Mamie!"

"But," she continues, "above all, your mother needs to agree."

My heart sinks, and Mamie knows why.

"Yes, you know how she can be; it isn't a sure thing."

"But you will help me convince her, right?"

Her answer is a kiss on my head as she keeps working.

Lost in my dreams of an escapade to the market, I hadn't noticed the significant progress that Mamie had made in her preparation. The remaining vegetables in the basket were now rid of their tops, washed, cut and floating in the cooking pot with some cold water and a small handful of sea salt. Dried white beans which Mamie had soaked overnight, have doubled in volume are drained, and thoroughly rinsed. A moment later, they join the vegetables.

"Hello, hello, are you awake?"

"Yes! Yes, Mamie! Everything smells so good!"

"Then tell me, what ingredient makes a real garbure?"

A few minutes of dreamy distraction have made me a fool. I don't know the answer. I feel my face blush.

Mamie smiles as a plume of smoke from her Marlboro escapes her nostrils.

"Without the Tarbais beans that only grow in the Pyrénées region, we do not have a real garbure. You'll remember this, Eric?"

"The Tarbais beans!"

"Grown where?"

9

"The Pyrénées!"

"Smart fellow."

Mamie constantly adds things to her soup: a heel of ham, a piece of preserved pork or duck meat, bay leaves, pepper. She also feeds the wood stove some logs and very soon we hear the fire crackling. The heat diffuses the fragrance of cabbage and leeks and spreads it throughout the three-room apartment.

She is a master. I am learning why Mamie is considered the queen of the garbure Béarnaise. Everyone relishes her soup, and it is well known to be the best in the region.

But I have my own reasons for naming the meal King Henry's Garbure.

THREE

Jean-Marc & Me

For a few hours, the soup simmers on one corner of the stove.

In the meantime, my brother Jean-Marc has arrived and we ask Mamie permission to go play outside. Our request is granted on the condition that we come back at 4 p.m. for a snack and don't leave the area.

We reply that we will be in the courtyard of the nearby Château de Pau. Mamie is proud of our French heritage, and loves that we consider Henry IV's castle our playground.

Upon arrival in the castle courtyard, the king's white marble statue welcomes us. He must love children, we assume, because he allows us to play in his home while watching us from up on high, apparently smiling under his beard.

The castle guards, on the other hand, are less understanding.

"You there! Yes, you! Stop. Stop it right now!"

They give chase with the intention of returning we rowdy brothers to the entrance, where they will lecture us about proper behavior — when they can catch us.

I confess, Jean-Marc and I do some stupid things, such as throwing stones in the condemned well of the central courtyard, or in the carp basin, and we often mingle among the tourists so that we can move past the guards undetected and into to the castle rooms, where we always raise a ruckus. We love this magnificent place and know it by heart.

The Mazère Tower, with its 1.7-meter-thick walls dating back to the 11th century, is the oldest part of the castle. One day, one of the nicer guards showed us a secret door inside the tower wall, and then forbade us to enter. For weeks afterward, we returned to the tower without our escort and attempted to find the passage again, without success.

In the course of history, other sections were added to the castle; a consequence of destruction and reconstruction. The castle would undergo other transformations as well but would owe its fame to the birth of the future king of France, Henry IV, in 1553.

It is said that Henry's grandfather, Henri d'Albret, baptized him according to the Béarn custom by rubbing his lips with a clove of garlic and making him breathe Jurançon wine from a goblet. Henry IV's baptismal cradle was a giant turtle shell that can still be seen in the king's bedroom in the castle.

King Henry IV was very popular in Béarn, and the Bearnese, aware of his fondness for food, made him crystallized fruits, pâtés, jams and other divine dishes, such as garbure or casseroled chicken with vegetables.

My God, it's already 4:30 p.m.!

My brother and I start running because Mamie must have already prepared our snack and we are starving. We run up the old, worn oak staircase, polished by time, but upon our arrival she sends us back to Madame Marchand, the baker on the ground floor, to buy sweetened dough pastries for our snack and bread for dinner.

We race back down because the bakery closes at 5 o'clock. We can't blame Mr. Marchand for an early closing time. After all, he starts baking in the middle of the night. But we are eager to fulfill our task because we don't like the baker's wife much. She scares us a bit, sometimes yells at us, especially when she catches us playing in the bake house. We nickname her Madame Double Chin, due to her imposing stature and the fat in her neck that forms a hefty fold and shakes when she moves.

Upon our return to Mamie's, the milk and sugar containers are on the table, and tea is about to be poured into big bowls. No formality necessary; we all help ourselves. At the bakery, Jean-Marc and I bought ourselves some pains au chocolat and an almond croissant for Mamie. Oh, my, it is delicious. We dunk our sweet pastries in our hot tea and carefully tap it on the rim of the china bowl before greedily gulping down mouthfuls. How we enjoy the soothing food!

Once satiated, we start playing a card game called belote to pass the time until dinner and, of course, Mamie is the winner!

Later, when the garbure's rich fragrance lures us from our game, the family gathers at the dinner table and we sit. I watch Grandmother ladle a generous portion from the tureen into my bowl. Then, eyes wide and mouth watering, this penniless boy from Ousse des bois picks up his spoon and experiences how it must feel to eat like a king.

FOUR

Momas,
a Small Bearnese Village

It is Sunday and my family is on its way to Momas to spend the day with Uncle Jean, Aunt Jeannette and their children. I love these visits. Their village in the Bearnese countryside is just thirty minutes from Pau. Yet there is a world of difference between our big-city suburb and their rural environment. The beautiful route prepares us for the transition.

I feel peaceful packed into the backseat of the car with my brother and sister when we reach the Boulevard Cami Sallié. It is lined for kilometers with huge 100-year-old plane trees that create a living, breathing canopy of green. The serenity deepens as we turn onto the equally rustic Avenue Chemin du Pont Long.

As we enter the quaint village I am reminded how small it is: it takes just a few minutes to cross from one end to the other. And there is only one local business — a bar that is located in front of the church.

The lone establishment opens only on Sundays after Mass, and for funerals, of course. Yet it remains closed after baptisms and communions, as these events are typically private and the meals and beverages are supplied by merry family members. So, you see, there wouldn't be enough clients to justify opening the bar, especially if the owner has been invited to the festivities.

City Hall is adjacent to the village center and church, which is itself adjacent to my uncle's land. Not long ago the new mayor had a tennis court built between the village center and my uncle's forge. What a scandal! This "modern" sport for important people doesn't impress my uncle who has always lived in this village without sidewalks or public lighting. And the mayor has only one tennis opponent — his wife.

I see my uncle and auntie's home with its green shutters, and a moment later Dad parks his car, a Renault 14, nicknamed "the pear" because of its shape. The kitchen curtains quiver. It is probably my cousin and godmother Monique, a well-informed gossip who has hurried to the window to see who is coming, a typical reaction when a car dares to drive across the village.

As the front door opens we jump out of the car. Enthusiastic hugs and kisses follow. But this can be dangerous. In Béarn, both men and women peck each other on the cheek four times. This is troublesome only when we must kiss Monique. We have learned to be careful because her chin is pointy and can hurt when, in a rush of loving salutations, her sharp chin smacks into our cheeks.

My Uncle Jean appears, smiling, arms wide. His forge is famous throughout the region and he is in high demand. There is always an agricultural machine to fix, a metal fence or a wrought-iron gate to make.

Sometimes during our visits I watch my uncle work in his workshop. It is fascinating and impressive to see him activate the enormous bellows on one side of the hearth to tease the fire and make the embers glow. The noise created by the bellows is loud, rhythmic and unique — "pfff... PFFFF...pfff." The sound is followed by crackling flames that devour heaps of coal that are shoveled in and quickly turned into the incandescent embers that heat the metal until it is red-hot. Only then can my uncle hammer the metal on the corner of the anvil and begin to shape it. Speed is essential because the iron can't cool down much before it is shaped. It is a very physical, difficult and tiresome work that has been handed down in this family from father to son for generations. Sadly this ritual will stop with Jean.

Jean's son Dédé, greets us. He has no interest in the forge. In fact, he hasn't

15

learned a trade of any kind. Instead, he spends a lot of time petting cats while sitting next to the fireplace and, in general, enjoying life by doing odd jobs on the farm. Mother says he isn't stupid — he's just lazy, a big sloth, she claims. But I like my cousin Dédé because despite being nearly 20 years older, he plays with us.

Monique, on the other hand, is the opposite of her brother. All week long she works outside of the village at a center for the disabled. She sells handmade objects and delivers meals and provides other services. She returns to Momas on the weekends to help her mother in the kitchen.

Aunt Jeannette is the boss of this small family and enterprise. She maintains the farm by caring for the garden and yard. Yet she also welcomes forge clients and farm visitors, and serves them red wine in a brandy glass in her kitchen. It seems that in the country, business dealings always end with a glass of wine.

While our sister Christine chats with Mom and Aunt Jeannette, Jean-Marc and I spend the morning playing in the vegetable garden and the farmyard with Dédé. We give him a hand filling old iron dishes with water for the poultry to drink; and helping him replace straw in the rabbits' hutch, remembering to pet the soft, cuddly animals at length. The chubby ones will soon be gone: they will provide a hearty meal in the farm kitchen, or travel with the poultry for sale at the Pau market.

We chase the guinea-fowls, ducks and turkeys a bit before we are scolded by Jeannette who surprises us when she arrives to choose a big, plump chicken. To halt further foolishness and make us useful, she suggests we feed the pigs.

We race to the kitchen to help Dédé pour soup for the pigs into a big pail. Jeannette and Mamie both make soup: a delicious concoction can almost always be found simmering on the stove top. But there is one significant difference: Mamie's soup is for her family, while Jeannette's is for the pigs.

Have pigs anywhere in the world ever dined so well?

To prepare the feast, my aunt collects all odds and ends — leftovers — in a big dish: meat scraps, vegetable peels, bread crumbs and crusts. These ingredients combine for a flavorful mishmash that helps fatten up the pigs. From September to January, each will gain about 100kg, if well fed. On this visit, we add some acorns and chestnuts to the soup because the pigs are fond

16

of them and it makes them grow faster.

In the stall, the swine greedily devour their meal. They always seem to have an appetite. Dédé tells me my uncle has retained the services of the slaughterer for January. He comes to the farm to kill, clean and butcher the pigs so that the family can make various products, such as sausages, ham and blood sausages.

After they are butchered, the pigs will be skinned and washed in hot water. Later they might be wrapped with straw and grilled according to regional tradition. Then they will be scraped with a knife to get rid of all remaining hair, and hung by their feet from a hook, head down, to be gutted and cleaned. The entrails will be used to make chitterlings and blood sausage. Other parts of the animal will be used to make various products such as cooked or cured hams, salamis made from Italian-style garlic-cured sausage, ventrêche (a type of cured pork belly), gras double (cooked tripe stew) and pâtés. That reminds me of a saying from Brittany: "From the tail to the chin, all is good in the pig." These words are also true in Béarn.

My body shudders at the idea of butchering the pigs. Yet, when I think of all the wonderful dishes that we regularly eat in Momas, I know the ordeal is necessary.

Indeed, what would life be like for the Bearnese without their famous blood pudding, one of the oldest-known cooked meats? The "pudding" is actually a mix of ingredients and dark brown sausage sold in meter-long pieces or in links tied at each end. Each pork butcher has his own recipe, which starts with pig's blood, herbs and spices. Although the recipes vary from region to region, they always include the lean and fatty meat of the pig, rind, onions, spices, blood, sugar, milk by-products, glutamate and seasonings.

Some recipes also call for spinach, grapes, apples, chestnuts, eau de vie, as well as bread and eggs; tasty additions, to be sure. But the most important ingredient in blood sausage, which the French call boudin noir, is the seasoning; it balances flavor when added with well-cooked onions.

Before all this can happen ham must be made. The process begins when pigs are slaughtered in late October or early November. Hams in the range of 8 to 9 kg (including bone) are washed and then rubbed in rock salt with black pepper and aromatic dry herbs, such as bay leaves, rosemary and thyme. Then they are placed into a large cheesecloth type of bag to protect them from

17

insects. Only then can they be hung to dry in a place where temperature, 6 to 8 °C, and humidity are controlled. This initial preserving process will last until the end of January or early February.

The next part of the process includes a mixture of pork fat and flour called 'pannage' which is used to seal the cut end of the joint. This reduces the speed in which the meat will dry during the warmer months of March, April and May. At some point during this period many of the ham producers will also rub a paste of Piment d'Espelette — a famous chili powder produced in the neighbouring Basque region — into the skin, giving a unique tang to the end product.

The final drying stage is completed by the end of July; at that time the ham is ready for consumption..

But I digress. Let's get back to the farm.

After feeding the pigs, we're famished. Thank God it is already snack time.

We head back to the farmhouse kitchen where Uncle Jean carves huge slices from a seven-pound loaf of bread with a very thick brown crust. The slices are toasted upright near the crackling flames in the fireplace. Moments later, with Dédé's help, Jean-Marc and I carefully turn them over so they don't burn. The smell of the toasted bread mixed with the smell of the fire is delectable.

The women — Mom, Mamie, Jeannette, Monique and little Christine — are in charge of preparing the tea and café au lait.

The table is cleared and the plastic table cloth is cleaned to make way for a variety of flavorful jars of jam and quince jelly. All the jams are homemade by Jeannette who comes into the dining room with a basket of cherries and a cake. She stretches out her arms and holds the basket of sweets in front of her like a trophy. Her smile grows radiant as she watches our eyes sparkle and grow wide with surprise. We can barely contain our craving for desserts.

The cake is a wonderful pastis Béarnais with some sablés, or shortbread biscuits. She didn't make the cake, but bought it from the baker who drove by in a van in the early morning, as is the custom in villages without shops. Some store owners and retailers from nearby villages, like the baker, make their rounds once or twice a week stopping in the village center and at farms, honking to

CHAPTER FOUR

make their presence known. That also explains the enormous proportions of the bread loaf, which must be kept as fresh as possible for several days until the baker returns.

Street peddlers also visit the village and are greeted by young people eager to buy candy, especially the Haribo Gummi Strawberries and the Hollywood-brand chewing gums they have seen advertised on television commercials.

As you can imagine, snack time in Momas is always a memorable experience. The pastis — not to be confused with the anise-flavored liqueur, is a kind of pastry made from raised dough— is soft, smooth and rich with the fragrance of vanilla. The toasted bread slices smeared with jam are a crunchy, aromatic delight. And Jeannette's shortbread biscuits are lightly golden with a buttery flavor that I like even better after dunking them in my tea or hot chocolate. Yes, the food is grand, but so is the joy we share as we savor the hearty treats together.

After our snack, Jean-Marc, Dédé and I run into the farm's large vegetable garden, careful not to step on decorative flowers. We play Hide-n-Seek, the Three Little Pigs and tag games. Then Dédé takes us to the barn to see the chicks and the ducklings in the incubator. We gently remove the cute creatures so we can stroke their soft feathers.

It goes without saying that in Pau we don't really have any contact with nature and animals, except when we go fishing — but who ever met a fish that liked to cuddle? Yuk!

As the chicks chatter —peep, peep, peep — I can't quite imagine that they will become big hens, roosters and ducks and, just like their parents, they will end up roasted or casseroled. Such is farm life.

I spot a big ladder on the side of the barn which leads to a loft. We aren't allowed to go up there because it is dangerous: planks are missing, broken or worm-eaten. Yet I'm young and foolish. I was born to explore.

With great speed and glee, I climb the ladder, which is very solid with big wooden rungs. When I reach the top, I can see that at least three quarters of the attic's floor surface is covered with corn kernels. I look over my shoulder at Dédé who is holding the ladder.

"Dédé, what's all this corn?"

"Well, it's corn," he replies.

"I know," I sigh. "But why is it there?"

Dédé doesn't answer my question directly.

"Don't go in there. You can't walk on it. You'll kill it if you walk on it; you'll smother the kernels by crushing them and they won't grow."

"I thought the corn was to feed the poultry."

"Yes, but not only. You see, it's the crop from both fields. We husk it to expose the ear. Then we put the corn in the corn drier and, after a couple of months, when all the moisture is gone, we remove half the kernels and that's what's in front of you now. We use it as feed for the animals and as seed for the next season."

"How do you remove the kernels?" I ask.

"Get down and I'll show you," Dédé says.

Dédé leads Jean-Marc and me to a large wooden box with a big funnel on top and a big wheel on the side.

"This machine separates the kernels from the ear of the corn," he explains. "You put the ears into the funnel. You turn the wheel and the kernels fall to one side and the ears to the other. We then take the kernels up to the attic to let them dry thoroughly since the part that was attached to the ear is still a bit humid and if we put it in a bag right away, it would rot and the crop would be destroyed."

As I stretch to glance in the funnel of the machine, Dédé goes on.

"Once it is dry, we will put it in bags and store it until we plant it next year. We have to manage the crop. You can't give it all to the ducks!" He laughs.

"What about the ears?" Jean-Marc asks.

20

"We let them dry out, too, and then use them as kindling in the fireplace."

At the time, the Monsanto Company with its transgenic kernels had not yet sparked a protest against genetically modified organisms (GMOs), which many farmers believe are a risk to the environment.

And so, as Dédé tutored his young cousins on the natural wonders of farm management, it was impossible to imagine then that years later a corn field in the middle of the countryside would be planted under government supervision, surrounded by barbed wire and, for a few months, daily safeguarded by the Republican Corps for Security (CRS), a national police division designed for civil protection.

It was also unreal to think that the minute the police had their backs turned, members of France's radical farmers' union, the Peasant's Confederation, under the leadership of José Bové, would destroy the genetically modified crop in protest. The defiance would get Bové arrested and imprisoned and turn him into a national hero. And even today, Bearnese farmers still actively resist this sly invader with its pollen that spreads to nearby fields on the wind.

Dédé, Jean-Marc, and I leave the barn and decide to continue our play by investigating the neighboring farm that belongs to the Landresse family.

"Oh, my, their farm is much bigger than ours," Dédé says. "They are owners of an industrial pigsty."

We are greeted by the two Landresse boys who are about the same age as Jean-Marc and me and who agree to take us on a tour of the pigsty. We are amazed by what we see.

The whole operation is nothing like Uncle Jean's farm. There are hundreds of pigs! This is not surprising, though, when you do the math. Ten good sows can bear 160 piglets a year if each one of them has two litters of eight.

We push open the door to the pigsty and are assailed by the smell and noise. This is definitely not the flowery, clean smell of the countryside. It stinks to high heaven!

On the other hand, although I have always heard that pigs are dirty I am impressed with the neatness of the pigsty.

We immediately go to see the sows lying down in their enclosure and the piglets running about all over. They are so cute, light pink with their small corkscrew tails, ears springing when they run. When we approach them, they raise their snouts towards us, snorting a bit, probably thinking we are going to give them bread crusts or an apple. Eating seems to be the only thing on their minds.

Next we go to the barn and cross the stable where the cows have been herded after spending the day in the field. Their udders are quite full and they are waiting to be milked in the big stable, lined up in their stalls, thirty animals on each side. As they present their backside, I laugh quite a bit with Jean-Marc. From the door, all we can see are two rows of enormous hindquarters.

The Landresse boys tell us their cows are Norman. These animals are distinguished by their "eyeglasses," the circular brown or white markings around their eyes. A Norman cow can produce up to thirty liters of milk a day, though the Landresse are happy with about twenty liters per day. A cow consumes a daily ration of sixty to eighty kilograms of forage and drinks thirty to ninety liters of water, depending on the humidity in the forage, the lactating period and the heat. A cow devotes eight hours a day to feeding its face, interrupted only by periods of serious rumination.

This farm is not only large, it is very modern for 1977. The cows are led to the fields to graze or to the stable to be milked according to a precise schedule, which is also dependent on the weather forecast.

Dédé is quite spirited while explaining that the Landresse have a traditional stable but with "hobbled" stalling. That is, each cow has its own stall with a straw bed, as well as drinking and feeding troughs.

The cows are milked twice a day in their own stall, where a good ventilation system provides lots of fresh air. The cows like the comfort of their stalls, especially when it is too hot or too cold outdoors. They can lie down on their cozy litter of straw and hay. As for the dairy calves, they are kept in a collective enclosure laid out in the middle of the stable like a nursery or a day care.

The cows enjoy a well-balanced feed mixture of forage, (pasture, silage and hay) and grains of barley or kernels of corn. They also get supplements aimed at optimizing their health and the quality of the milk they produce.

Dédé grabs a stool and asks if we would like to milk one of the cows. We crack up laughing as he gives us a demonstration.

He looks at me and says, "Don't be scared, Eric."

"I'm not scared."

"Yes you are," Jean-Marc chimes in.
"No I'm not!"

We scuffle a bit and then laugh, which helps me hide the fact that I am a little scared.

Dédé carries on. "You see, if you're scared or nervous — "

"I'm not."

"He's not!" Jean-Marc smirks.

"I know you're not. But if you were, she will feel it and will be scared too. So we'll treat her right. First we need to wash her udder with a wet cloth."
"Is that utterly necessary," Jean-Marc quips.

Dédé grins and hands me a cloth. "Here you go."

I hesitate.

"Come on, Eric."

"Oh okay," I say and set myself up exactly as my cousin instructed. To prove I'm not afraid, I quickly reach for the udder with the cloth and —

"But slowly."

"Okay, okay."

"The udder is sensitive. The cow's teats are full now and they hurt. But after we wash her, the milking will relieve the pain!"

Pain?

23

All these instructions and my nearness to the large animal have deflated me; I am not so cocky. After all, the cow is more than twenty times my weight, and if she is in pain, one kick would send me flying across the stable.

Dédé continues his tutoring.

"Put this bucket underneath a teat. Good. Now, take the teat between your thumb and index finger and move it back and forth, and up and down, lightly pressing the end as you pull it down. Each time, the milk will come out in powerful sprays. You understand?"

I grunt and nod, a little tense, and then gingerly do as told. The first shot of milk hits the bottom of the pail and, to me, sounds like thunder. I'm elated.

"I am milking a cow!"

"My turn!" Jean-Marc shouts.

"Not yet!"

"My turn, scaredy-cat!"

Dédé quiets us and whispers: "Don't scare her. There is plenty of milking to do."

Despite our little lesson, the Landresse don't milk by hand anymore. They have begun using an electric milking machine. It's unique in the village of Momas and one of the reasons this farm family is considered rich.

They are also very nice. They have worked hard for their wealth, and have grown by keeping up with changing trends and modernizing as much as possible.

We thank the Landresse boys for the tour and wave goodbye, and then run to Auntie Jeannette's for dinner.

Our meal is simple but delicious. A light soup with vegetables from the garden, an egg prepared sunny-side up with shingar, a local type of rolled pancetta, a big lettuce, also from the garden, and a generous piece of cheese from the Pyrénées.

When we are well satisfied, we say our goodbyes and thanks and pile into our car, putter through the village and then turn onto the tree-lined roads that will lead us back home.

The country air has served us well. The farmland has provided a relaxing respite from the concrete environment of home. I doze off in the car as I think about my exciting day, and all the animals I touched, petted and milked. We kids often are scolded by the adults who believe we are annoying all the wonderful farm creatures. But what child can resist chasing a flock of chickens or cuddling a baby pig? In the city we don't have these warm, intimate encounters with nature — How do you embrace concrete? — and so we invade the rural community at full tilt. Maybe it is disruptive. But young people first live through their senses; the intellect develops later.

I awaken when Dad stops the car in front of Mamie's place near Pau Castle. We kiss our grandmother and say good night.

"I'll see you on Wednesday, dear ones," Mamie reminds us.

Tomorrow is a school day. Back to my routine: breakfast, bus, school, cafeteria, bus, house, homework, dinner and sleep.

Already I'm looking forward to my Wednesday visit with Mamie. City life is not so bad.

CHAPTER FOUR

FIVE

The Technique of the
Warm Cupboard

I am a boy who absorbs information and personalities with the same ease and enthusiasm as bread absorbs milk and tea, I know the difference between Mamie and Auntie Jeannette by the way they run their kitchens; the meals they provide their loved ones reflect their personalities. I soak it all up.

My mother's kitchen is also unique, especially her method of preparing meals and keeping them warm. Her technique produces interesting results that are worth mentioning. Yet this little boy also knows that her approach has been shaped by her significant limitations.

Mother's health is chronically weak and so she must stay at a clinic for rest and recuperation, usually twice a year.

When our mother is home, she is obsessed with cleaning because she fears filth of any kind will further erode her quality of life. Her constant need to wash every surface and rid everything of dust means the air is heavy with the scent of disinfectant and the wax she uses to polish the furniture and floors.

It isn't just the smell we children dislike. Our mother's cleaning habits remind us of the shoe brushes we own that can be worn like sandals. When our mother punishes us for our childish indiscretions, she makes us don this footwear to wax and polish the floor with the motion of our feet.

In any case, the cleaning (or the act of disciplining her lambs) so compromises her vigor that meal preparation is a long, tedious procedure that starts very early in the day, rarely varies, and ends with mediocre, tasteless results. My brother, sister and I bear in mind the circumstances, and believe Mother is probably doing her best. But our sensitivity to her plight does not entirely quell our disappointment in the evening meal. It may even heighten our anticipation of breakfast the next morning.

When our school days start, usually about 7 a.m., we may be tired but we know our taste buds will quickly awaken because, before waking us, Dad prepares our breakfast.

We all gather together around the kitchen table with hot chocolate for the kids and café au lait for my parents. Prominently displayed in the center of the table are two big plates of biscottes that glisten with a layer of butter and jam. Dad's handiwork.

Boy, do I eat a lot of biscottes! (Maybe I didn't eat enough dinner the night before.) Often we buy them in huge packets of two hundred and fifty, or ten cartons of twenty-five. We fill the pantry.

"Eric is hogging the biscottes!" my sister complains.

I protest. "Am not!"

"Are, too!" Jean-Marc says as he reaches across me to grab another for himself.

Biscottes are bread slices cooked until golden and then dried in the oven. They are fragile and crumbly, especially when you try to spread hard butter on them which may cause them to explode in your hand, unless you know a couple tricks of the trade. For instance, when using cold butter, create a strong base by stacking two biscottes, one on top of the other — to avoid them breaking into a million pieces.

Our favorite jam is usually homemade by Mamie, quince jelly or apricot jam,

27

or Aunt Jeannette, who favors strawberries or figs. Regardless of the topping, the best part is yet to come: devouring our delicious morning meal.

The art of eating a biscotte when you are twelve years old is to dunk it lightly in your cup of hot chocolate, just long enough for it to absorb enough liquid to make it spongier, but not so much that it losses its slight crunch and disintegrates into the cup. This comes with practice. Lots of practice.

Many people think the French eat croissants for breakfast every day. But generally those divine buttery, flakey pastries are reserved for Sundays or special occasions. So, should you visit France, don't be surprised by the prominent display and size of the biscottes packages in the supermarket, especially the so-called family portions. And don't be shocked by the many types that are available!

✳✳✳

Mom never actually cooks. She buys cold cuts from the caterer, soups in packets, salamis, pâtés and rillettes, canned raviolis, canned vegetables, prepared meals, cheeses and yogurts.

She generally starts preparing lunch at around 7 a.m. and dinner around 1 p.m. To keep the coffee pot clean, she only makes coffee once a week.

Our gas cooker, purchased fifteen years ago, is still essentially new for lack of use; regardless, mom cleans it twice a day.

Fortunately, we have a microwave oven which has practically saved our lives. But before this marvelous invention arrived at our house, my mother had an unusual technique for heating up meals without dirtying the gas stove.

We called it the technique of the warm cupboard!

The warm cupboard is a tiny room in our apartment like an old washroom without windows. At the bottom of the cupboard, hot water pipes from the building's central heating system line the wall. The heat emanating from the pipes is sufficient to bathe this tiny room in a soothing warmth, ergo the nickname "the warm cupboard."

My mother's technique consists of heating up a stewpot half filled with

28

CHAPTER FIVE

water, in which she places a Pyrex dish. In the dish she places canned vegetables on one side, and on the other, meat slices bought at the supermarket. She covers the dish with a plate, and puts everything on the stove until the water boils for thirty minutes. Voila! This is what we call double boiling.

As the stewpot heated up, Mom would spread a worn-out sheet on the kitchen table, fold it in four and put it on an old wash towel. After the stewpot had boiled, she would rest it on the towel, then fold the four corners of the sheet over it and tightly close everything with safety pins. This unique bundle would then be placed against the pipes in the cupboard to keep warm until served. The temperature is ideal for the development of microbes. My brother Jean-Marc and I grow up to joke that we were brought up on bacteria — "We can handle it!"

But the warm cupboard method was not limited to processed meats and canned foods.

Imagine the horror of eating eggs sunny side up that had been prepared in this way. Let's repeat Mom's process, in case you wish to try this at home. (Please don't!)

In the morning, break the eggs into a Pyrex shallow plate — no frying required

Cover eggs and cook in a double boiler for 30 minutes

Wrap eggs in a large towel and place in the warm cupboard

At lunch remove the eggs, now thoroughly overcooked and nauseating to look at because what should be a messy yellow glory of soft yokes now looks no more appealing than a plate of round, plastic drain covers.

Now for the bread, not that there is any tasty goo to wipe from our plates. I bring it up to illustrate that Mom's kitchen techniques extend beyond the limits of the warm cupboard.

Once again, cleanliness is the objective. To avoid unsavory bread crumbs that would taint her immaculate kitchen, Mother cuts the loaves every two or three days into individual slices and keeps them in a bag fastened with clothesline pegs, a precursor to Ziploc plastic bags.

CHAPTER FIVE

It only takes a few hours for the good crusty bread purchased from Mr. Méchain, our local baker, to devolve into a rubbery slab that needs to be chewed vigorously for several minutes before being swallowed.

Bon appétit!

✳✳✳

Bless her soul, but Mother's kitchen manner is confusing; I am not old enough to fully comprehend. The products she buys are not necessarily the least expensive. The caterer's prepared meals, for example, cost far more than the produce available at the local market. Even a child might figure out that a little preparation at meal time and some fresh, aromatic vegetables every once in a while could go a long way toward improving our unpleasant menu.

I know Father feels the same way because, despite his long, arduous work days, sometimes he brings home a roast beef and carrots, or prepares a rabbit in mustard. O Holy Night! Real food served as a respite from our normally listless, unappetizing diet.

Even though I am a child, I quickly learn to differentiate home meals from the greedy pleasures served by others, such as Mamie or Auntie and in the homes of friends.

In an odd way, Mother's lack of joie de vivre in the kitchen was formative. It became evident that I would need to become a chef if I wanted to reproduce the succulent dishes that I discovered during the numerous snacks and meals at Mamie's, in Momas, or with my other aunt Jeannette d'Aramits (one more of Dad's cousins who we lovingly refer to as "aunt") during our Sunday excursions in the beautiful Pyrénées.

Soon my goal is to emulate Mamie: I too want to be a magician with food. I will unlock the secrets that hide in rich, generous and abundant sauces. I will make an inventory of creamy desserts; and blend herbs, condiments and spices so that I might experience (and never forget) a galaxy of new flavors.

My choice is to familiarize myself with the food profession, which I've only glimpsed and yet seems so full of delectable promises. I want to know everything, learn it all and, in turn, become the grand master of what we call the culinary art!

30

In later years at cooking school, I will develop skills and gain the technical know-how that is an essential part of becoming a chef. But without Mamie ...

Grandmother's teaching and hearty helpings might have led to mere gluttony or piggish glee. On the contrary, her intelligence and patience subtly lead me to appreciate the soulful pleasures of cooking. How lucky I am to witness the amazing alchemy between the spiritual and material aspects of food preparation, especially during our walks through the farmers market. I glean that the creation of delicious, life-affirming meals demands more than a mix of good products.

By way of example, Mamie helps me discover that the main ingredients in her fabulous treats all come from her heart.

A warm cupboard of love, passion, care and generosity.

CHAPTER FIVE

SIX

Excursion to Les Halles

I wake up in Mamie's bed and realize today is the big day! It is Saturday, the beginning of Spring vacation. Usually I would rather sleep late, but not on this wonderful morning. I am excited and happy because Mother finally agreed to let me spend the night so that I can accompany Grandmother to the market — a special wish finally come true.

I rise and quickly bathe. Jean-Marc and my sister Christine will join us in the afternoon because Mamie has promised to make crepes. Until then, it is just me and my grandmother.

We leave the house around quarter past eight, but instead of going directly to Les Halles, we begin what seems to be a ritual for Mamie.

First, we meet the neighbor next door, Mrs. Mendes, who holds out her selection for betting on today's horse races; these bi-weekly events take place in Paris. The locals place bets through Pari Mutuel Urbain, the national betting system, after reading a racing form that assigns a number to each mount.

We then stop by the bakery. Mr. Méchain is also waiting for us, certain, as usual, that he has chosen a winning combination of numbers. Grandmother places his bets for him because he is too busy baking and cannot leave his shop.

With half a pain au chocolat — called chocolate croissant in North America — in hand (the other half makes my cheeks bulge as the delicious, buttery pastry slowly melts in my mouth), I cross the square with my grandmother and we stop by the Café Gascon. Mamie talks with everyone, especially the owner, about the races and the numbers to play. No one seems to agree.

We walk some more and stop to see Mrs. Brouca, the pork butcher's wife, who calls to the back of the shop, asking her husband for advice. Mamie and Mrs. Brouca discuss horses, races to come, and last week's results in Longchamp, the famous Parisian race course.

Once the race card has been decided, Mr. Brouca hands us a small piece of toast that is topped with graisserons, a delicious mix of duck and pork cooked in fat. While the adults chatter, I wander around the store. I have the whole place to myself because Mr. Brouca does not officially open until 9 a.m.

Mamie has told me that Mr. Brouca moved here more than fifty years ago when he began to earn a reputation as a great pork butcher. His products are numerous and delicious. Hams, salamis and rolled-up ventrèches hang from the ceiling. The shelves overflow with tins bearing his name; the descriptions of the contents make my mouth water: pork terrine with apricots, boar pâté with Cognac, duck and pork rillettes, liver mousse in port wine, foie-gras au naturel semi-cooked in Armagnac and the exclusive house-brand tripes à la mode.

The shop windows also are bursting with beautifully displayed items. The choice of pâtés is amazing. A dozen types of terrines are laid out before my eyes, some round and nicely decorated. The duck rillettes, molded into the shape of a duck, are not presented in a bowl but on a stainless steel tray. As for the pork rillettes, they are shaped into a pig's head. It is incredibly artistic! The white hams prepared by the charcutier are round and imposing, their rind thick and shiny, their slices pink and juicy. The raw hams still have a pig's foot attached, the huge hoof nail resembles a polished precious stone.

The display of prepared meals is every bit as enticing; I can't help but go around behind the counter for a closer look. While the adults engage in a lively discussion that rises and falls like a verbal symphony, I hide from their view and plunge my index finger into the dishes and sample   coq au vin, boeuf bourguignon and blanquette de veau. Even though the sauces are cold, the flavors and aromas, rich and subtle, ingenious and robust, invade my being and conquer my palate. I am a prisoner, a slave to sneaky taste tests. I am so

CHAPTER SIX

overwhelmed I'm in no hurry to leave.

Nevertheless, we leave the butcher shop with new race bets in hand and make a quick stop at the grocer's, but only to say hello. He gives me a beautiful clementine from Morocco with the leaves still attached to the stem. The clementine is juicy, refreshing and very sweet.

We then walk along the magnificent Queen Margaret Square to get to the café where the betting tickets are sold. To validate the tickets we must go to the far end of the café, an area that is smoky, crowded, stinky and disgusting with the smell of stale tobacco. Mamie introduces me to everyone and then leaves to play the numbers, hers and the ones entrusted to her by her neighbors and friends. Her lucky numbers are 2-5-8, and each is assigned to a horse that is predicted to lose.

"Why would you bet on losers, Mamie?"

"The payout will be quite nice."

"For losers?"

She laughs.

"No, silly, only if they win, because no one expects them to win."

"But you do?" I ask.

"They're long shots."

"Long shots in Longchamp?"

She laughs again, and I buzz with joy: I am so entertaining.

"We'll keep our fingers crossed. I'm playing the odds."

Odds. A difficult concept for this boy to understand.

After nearly an hour of lively discussion, we leave the café and are finally on the road to the market. We go down rue des Cordeliers to turn off on rue Tran and then rue Saint Jacques to finally arrive at Les Halles.

On this particular day, the market is swarming with city folk and country people of all ages, shapes and sizes. Some wear fine clothes; others are draped in drab overalls with sweaty caps pulled over their brows. They haul big baskets of produce and other food stuffs, and haggle over price or shout salutations to familiar faces. It is a carnival of commerce, a circus of oversized voices and characters. It is a thrill to be among them.

Mamie, who seems to recognize everyone, holds my hand and tells me to stay close to her for she could easily lose me. She greets faces here and there as shopkeepers call out to show us an item or hand us a food sample. We devour a piece of cheese on the left, a piece of apple on the right, a grape, pâté and so forth. All the products are amazing. The mix of aromatic and textured edibles and the electricity of the crowd are intoxicating and magical. I am dizzy with excitement.

The market is organized into sections: equine butchers, pork butchers, regular butchers, fishmongers, market gardeners, bakers, dry good merchants, pastry cooks, wine merchants and florists. Mamie points out an impressive display at a greengrocer stall, but says she would rather buy produce in the fruit and vegetable section.

"But why? All this food looks so delicious!"

"The same products are less expensive, and we'll buy directly from farmers just like those we visit in Momas."

This is thrilling. Maybe I'll recognize the farmers.

As we stroll from row to row, my eyes roam in all directions; I would like to taste, touch and smell everything. We finally arrive at the produce section — and I am a bit surprised.

This portion of the market is, in fact, a basketball court that is missing hoops at both ends. I know this because the concrete surface is painted green and marked with red and white lines. This space has been transformed into an annex of the permanent market so that local farmers can truck in their fresh produce.

The makeshift area is teeming with farmers, shoppers, kids my age, and others just taking a stroll. A cacophony of voices, bleats and squawks fills the air because, in addition to the vegetables, fruits, nuts and eggs that are on sale, small farmyard animals, including chickens and rabbits, are on show.

The farmers are proud and polite. They greet each passer-by and answer endless questions and offer advice about specific varieties of the fruits and vegetables they sell.

Mamie talks to a vegetable seller in the Bearnese regional dialect. The discussion is lively, but I don't understand any of it, except for a few words when they are referring to me.

"The little one ...."

"Ah. Yes. My grandson."

Mamie grabs a bunch of leeks, two large onions, some carrots and turnips and I learn that the farmer comes from Lescar, a village close to Momas. I'm delighted.

"Mamie, are the vegetables for the garbure ?" I ask.

"No, they are for the poule au pot."

"What's a poule au pot?"

"It is a stuffed hen stewed with vegetables. It is a very good and nourishing meal. As a matter of fact, our kind King Henry IV wanted all the French to be able to eat a poule au pot on Sundays so we are going to do what he says."

"Oh, boy. It's going to be delicious with all these vegetables."

"While I am thinking about this," Mamie says, "come on, Eric, we are going to choose a chicken."

"But Mamie, look. There are plenty of them here in this section."

"Yes, true. But these chickens and ducks are alive."

"Like in Momas!"

"Right again. But I don't want to kill a chicken myself. It's too messy."

"Yuk!" I say.

Mamie is always right.

Mr. Jean is a poulterer, which means he only sells poultry and products derived from — guess what? —poultry. Mamie quickly glances at the display and finds a bird she likes. It is a beautiful hen with a firm chest and milky, taut skin. It has just been eviscerated, that is to say all its entrails have been removed except for the liver, the heart, the gizzard and the eggs. Mr. Jean is proud of the products he sells.

"My chickens almost always have two eggs inside. They are raised outdoors and they are the partners of a very strong rooster."

He winks and grins. All the adults in the shop laugh. I am mystified. What's so funny?

With a couple of full baskets, we begin our trek home. But Mamie is hungry and wants to stop to have lunch in a restaurant. I willingly follow because I am hungry too, despite all the delicacies I sampled at the market.

The restaurant Mamie takes me to is actually a municipal cafeteria for the elderly. That suits Mamie just fine because she is proud to bring her grandchildren in and introduce them to her friends and acquaintances. This is not my first visit so I am familiar with the menu, and I always choose my favorite dish: a pan-fried freshly ground beef patty , cooked rare and accompanied by a generous heap of French fries. I can't get enough pommes frites!

Mamie continues her introductions as we sit at a big table where men and women chat loudly with one another. Some people I already know because I have been here before. To my right, I hear a conversation about horse racing, and to my left the lotto is all the rage. Soon the talk strays to other topics such as local politics and municipal support for the elderly. These are not conversations for a kid my age and I am somewhat bored so I slip out of my seat with a ticket to choose a dessert at the counter.

Since the choices are few it doesn't take very long for my eyes to scan the compote containers, flans, and cheese and fruit baskets before stopping at the mousse au chocolat. I had already spotted it when we were choosing our meal. Chocolate! It's a no-brainer for a boy.

But I guess I got carried away, because when I return to our table Mamie scowls.

"Licking the container again?"

I'm shocked. How did she know?

"No, Grandmother."

Mamie scowls a second time and quickly swipes my nose with a huge handkerchief that now reveals traces of chocolate.

Caught!

"It just isn't done, my lovely."

"But it's so good!"

Bad manners." And then she whispers, "Especially in public."

I grin and blush.

We return to Mamie's apartment in the early afternoon. After four hours at the market, I am among the walking dead. I drag myself to Mamie's bedroom for a nap.

I always find the bed a bit strange. It is covered with a huge comforter which must be at least twenty-five centimeters thick and yet barely covers the sides of the mattress. Despite its thickness, it hardly weighs a thing because it is made of down and small duck feathers that sometimes poke through the material and tickle my thin skin.

When I curl up underneath the swath of comfort, the warmth and lightness are as pleasant as a summer breeze. My body feels as though it is wrapped in a cloud and hovering above the floorboards. Deep sleep brings dreams of clucking farmyard animals, the charcutier, thoroughbreds and jockeys, the orange meat of a clementine, chattering elderly faces and mousse au chocolat smeared over every silly face! I am laughing in my sleep, as content as can be, until a bolder falls from above and crushes me.

"Ouch!"

My eyes pop open and I see Jean-Marc jumping on me. I complain, and the mattress springs groan, too. When my brother will not heed my cry I assault him with a pillow. A moment later Jean-Marc's pillow hits me broadside. We are fully engaged, with duck feathers flying, when Mamie arrives, a Marlboro hanging from the corner of her mouth.

"Get into the kitchen, you bandits!"

"But I'm winning the pillow fight," Jean-Marc insists.

"Are not!"
　　"Are too! You should have seen your face when I — "
Mamie is serious. "Get into the kitchen. Now!"

The pillow-fighting brothers run, with Mamie in hot pursuit, smoke literally billowing out of her nostrils.

We arrive in the kitchen and discover Mamie has been making crepes; they are piled high on a plate. We are forbidden to touch the crepes except for the failed ones that have been set aside on a dish. The pile keeps on growing as the level of the batter in the bowl slowly and steadily decreases. With each new crepe, Mamie stirs the batter with a ladle to keep it from separating since the flour has a tendency to settle at the bottom of the bowl. Mamie tells me to listen to the sound of the batter as she fills up the ladle and pours it back into the bowl.

"Your crepe batter needs to be light, smooth and without lumps. That's why I make it with milk and water. When you pour it out of the ladle with a level forearm, it must make a light sound, like a trickle of water running down. If your batter is too thick, the sound is coarser, thicker and heavier."

I ask, "Why does it matter?"

"The heavier the batter, the thicker the crepes, and the less you will have to eat."

"Oh, then it is serious! Make the batter light, Mamie, because I want to eat tons of crepes!"

Mom and our sister Christine arrive a bit later, after shopping on the rue Serviez and at Les Nouvelles Galeries, a mall full of fashion and novelty stands. They are a bit tired from having shuffled about the stores for most of the day.

Mom takes jars of jam, Nutella and honey out of the cupboard and serves tea in the living room. Mamie comes in with a humongous pile of crepes that everyone admires. In this wonderful atmosphere, I relate in great detail my adventure at the market with Mamie, while alternatively swallowing a crepe with strawberry jam, one with Nutella, another with quince jelly, and then finally a large crepe stuffed with Nutella, honey and banana slices. Oh, my. Should my indelicate eating manners give me a belly ache, I won't mind. More crepes, I say. More crepes!

Mamie asks me if I would like to help prepare the poule au pot for Sunday lunch.

"Of course!" I answer with my mouth full.

I am now completely bewitched by the secrets of preparing sumptuous, frivolous and serious food and I will not miss an opportunity to cook with my Mamie. Not for anything!

SEVEN

La Poule au Pot

E veryone else in my family has plans for Saturday afternoon. My brother leaves for his running club, Les Aigles de Pau; my sister meets with friends; and Dad travels to a construction site, a fact of life for a laborer who must work weekends to help pay for his children's education.

Fine with me. I have Mamie all to myself as she removes the central hotplate from her wood stove so that she can add a couple of dried logs to the dying embers. I see yellow flames rapidly hop and dance through the stove top opening.

Before reaching for the poultry, Grandmother entrusts me with one of her secrets for making excellent poule au pot: Always buy a mature chicken, but not more than two years of age, otherwise the flesh will be too tough.

Mamie takes the chicken out of the refrigerator and plucks the few visible feathers left on the bird. Once that task is done, she grabs the feet with one hand and the head with the other and swiftly stretches the chicken across the leaping flames, which lick the skin and burn off any remaining down feathers. The operation is tricky because some parts of the chicken are hard to reach, like between the feet or under the wings; and it must be done rapidly so that the skin isn't scorched.

The smell of charred feathers quickly fills the kitchen with a light, acrid and

41

unpleasant smoke. I rush to the window and open it to clear the air. Once the chicken is singed, Mamie places it on the cutting board and then with the help of a hook, she pulls the stove's cast iron hotplate back into place and the flames vanish.

With the chicken resting on one side, Grandmother chops off the feet two centimeters below the joint. Now it is time to behead the chicken.

The throat is cut at its base, carefully leaving the skin attached to the bird's abdomen. Then with a very sharp knife that I'm not allowed to touch, Mamie opens the neck and pulls away the fatty skin so that she can remove the esophagus. She must do this before entirely disconnecting the neck from the bird's rib cage. The esophagus is then discarded.

"Were you watching, Eric?"

How could I not watch Mamie's every movement? She is a master with knives.

"Yes, Mamie."

"Can you see why we must clean the neck bone?"

"Um…because necks are icky?"

She laughs and tells me my answer is partially correct.

"We clean the neck so that it can be added to the broth for extra flavor."

"But what about all that neck skin you cut off?"

"Ah. Wise child."

Mamie reaches for the excess skin and begins to apply a portion across the opening where the neck was removed. Another piece of skin is draped like a cape over the bird's back. Both actions added an extra layer of fat and a bit of protection. No one likes overcooked fowl.

Next, Mamie runs her finger around the base of the wishbone in the thoracic cage to release the membranes, the crop and the lungs; then she empties the innards of the bird. The giblets come out all at once, followed by two soft and yellowy masses that appear to be eggs without their shells. All is thrown out except for the gizzard, the liver and the heart.

It's like a horror movie. Blood, gizzards, hearts — and I am fascinated by all these preparations!

"My mother," says Mamie, "used to keep the hen's eggs — yes, those yellowy things are eggs. She'd put them in the stuffing. But I prefer using freshly laid eggs."

"I agree, Mamie." I try to make my comment sound mature, but really all I am thinking is, Yuck! How gross is that to use unformed eggs in your cooking!

She smiles, probably reading my mind: fresh eggs look far more appetizing.

I'm thrilled that Mamie wants me to prepare the vegetables. She gives me her basket in which there are carrots, leeks, two stalks of celery, some turnips, two onions and a small green cabbage. She instructs me to wash and peel them while she prepares the stuffing.

In a French kitchen there are strict rules for washing food. The root vegetables, all those that grow underground, must be scrubbed in cold running water to remove excess soil. They are then dropped in a cold bath that includes a drop of bleach. This kills all bacteria and toxins that might otherwise cause botulism or other diseases. Nasty, nasty. This procedure was a must in the old days, and is still an important precaution in today's world of organically grown food.

Leafy vegetables that grow above ground, such as lettuce, kale, and cabbage, are given their own bath in cold water with a drop of vinegar. This acidic mixture removes any insects that may be crawling within the layers of the leaves; they curl and drop to the bottom of the bath. Before discarding the filthy water, the clean food must be removed by hand and placed in a colander.

Lots of work for an eager boy like me!

"All nice and clean?" Mamie asks.

"Yes."

"Excellent. Now we'll use the vegetables to prepare a stock. When it's done, we'll keep it in the refrigerator overnight and then tomorrow use the stock to stew the chicken for our Sunday lunch."

43

Per Mamie's instructions, I place the veggies in a pot of cold water and then somehow successfully move the heavy burden to the stove.

When Grandmother begins cleaning up, I protest, "But we're not done!"

"Yet we've had a full day, haven't we?"

I agree. And maybe I'm just a little sleepy from all the exciting events.

Mamie explains that a delicious poule au pot can certainly be prepared in a day. But it can turn into an ordeal if you also go to market as we did, and then visit with friends and family.

"We'll get up early tomorrow and finish our work. It's easier for the chef and her assistant that way."

I love my new title: assistant to the master chef.

A simple dinner, storybook time and then I fall into Mamie's big bed and drop off to dreamland where I am chased in a House of Horrors by a headless chicken and fend off an army of giblets with a sword (actually, a very long carrot).

The next morning I wake up when I hear Mamie call. I dash to the kitchen.

In a big bowl, Mamie starts a panada by dipping stale bread leftovers into a glass bowl of milk with a hint of Cognac. She kneads everything so that the pieces of bread soak up every last drop of the liquid.

Then she places the bowl under a heavy mechanical meat grinder screwed to the edge of the kitchen table. First she adds and grinds the chicken liver, then the heart and a big veal scallop. To this, she adds a piece of regional raw ham (a portion of a cured ham prepared by Aunt Jeannette in Momas); a piece of ventrêche that has been salt cured and air dried, not smoked (also from Jeannette); and garlic, shallots and parsley.

I watch closely as Mamie adds salt, pepper, thyme and two eggs to the bowl and mixes everything for a few minutes more before stuffing the chicken. With a trussing needle, she sews the opening shut to prevent the stuffing from pouring out.

CHAPTER SIX

The chicken is immersed in the now warm stock where it will simmer on the stove at low heat for two hours.

"Have we forgotten anything?" Mamie asks.

I'm puzzled. What else could we possibly need?

"Remember the neck we cleaned yesterday?"

"For extra flavor!"

"Good boy!"

She adds the chicken neck to the pot, and from time to time skims the stock and tends to other kitchen tasks. This is when Mamie enjoys telling me more about King Henry IV, and repeating why he was called "the kind king."

If Mamie did not live in the old neighborhood so close to Château de Pau, the king's castle, perhaps her history lessons would be less frequent. Yet, as a family, we took great pride in being so close to such a significant historic site. And I'm sure the stories Mamie told helped me deepen my appreciation of France's traditions and rituals.

Also, every tale was a subtle reminder that the virtues of kindness, good humor and compassion must never be forgotten, no matter how high your position in life. Henry was royalty, yes, but this did not diminish his love of people, and for that reason his reign had a long and lasting impact on France.

And his love of food had a lasting impact on my family, as expressed through Mamie's generous meals and lessons.

As Mamie's long history lesson ends, Mother and my brother and sister arrive for their Sunday meal.

Mamie sends me to the cellar to get a new bottle of wine, giving me precise instructions because Mamie's bottles don't have any labels. The bottle is a Madiran that the wine maker sends directly to her. I am too young to drink wine, but not to eat poule au pot.

Dad arrives. As I mentioned, he has a full-time job during the week with Ganchou, a construction company in Pau. But he has been working for a private client, building a house on weekends and sometimes evenings when the weather is mild. He does this to earn extra money to help cover the cost of private school. I believe this is part of the reason Mamie cooks for us so much. She likes to be surrounded by her grandchildren, but she also likes to see her son and know that he is well fed.

Dad is starving. No surprise. But he must settle for the aperitif that is served while Mamie strains some broth from the poule au pot into a separate pan to which she adds fine angel hair pasta. The broth with pasta is our appetizer and it is delicious. Its golden, luxurious texture exudes a strong aroma, and the fatty beads that appear on the surface render the dish supple and sophisticated.

I explain the importance of including the neck in the stock preparation. But Jean-Marc smirks and says shut up and eat.

The appetizer has been consumed and our bellies are warm. Now we are ready for the coronation.

The poule au pot Mamie and I prepared is not something the French enjoy every day or even every month. It is on par with a visit from royalty. In other words, it is a time to rejoice.

We are silent when Grandmother arrives from the kitchen carrying the bird on a platter. As she sets down the meal, we gush, gawk and applaud as the intoxicating steam from the beautiful food rises like a sacrament and then floats down under our noses. We inhale and are overcome with desire: the aromas fill our senses, much like great music or a Renaissance painting endows us with the magnificence of life.

I am dizzy as I look upon the gleaming, plump breast and the exquisite vegetables, all so full of color, because I am seeing it with new eyes: I helped prepare this gastronomic delight and this simple fact excites me almost as much as the thought of consuming it.

The communal climax of our family soiree happens when Dad carves the chicken and serves each of us a generous piece with a slice of stuffing, some vegetables and the heaven-sent broth.

The meal is divine.

The delicate, lightly aromatic flesh of the bird melts in my mouth. The richly

46

fragrant panada emits ample and sumptuous perfumes that make my taste buds tingle in a frenzy of anticipation. First, I notice the supple texture of the soft part of the bread, engorged with the juice of the poultry liver; and once I chew and swallow a mouthful, it leaves a warm aftertaste with a hint of Cognac that brings a flush to my cheeks — a sensation I relish and will long remember. The vegetables deliver various essences and mouth-watering satisfaction without overpowering the flavor of the meat.

What a weekend for me! Unforgettable. Far from my family's low-cost housing, I have enjoyed so many experiences: Spending the night at Mamie's home so that I could shop with her the next day in Les Halles, where we sampled delicacies and met many interesting people. And beforehand, the tour of Pau when Grandmother collected horse bets. She didn't win at the races, but my kind, generous Mamie was a big hit with the many people she helped along the way.

Also a two-day cooking class that resulted in a masterful (and memorable) family Sunday meal.

It is with full stomachs and in a festive mood that my family returns home. In my room, lying on my bed, I replay and reflect on the images and highlights of the weekend, taking stock of it all.

I love to cook with Mamie, but the school year is coming to an end, and that means our family discussions have turned to summer vacation. We are probably going to go to the beach at Port-Vendres, like every year. I'm not complaining: Jean-Marc and I have a fun time by the sea.

Yet it saddens me a bit when I consider that the vacation will keep me so far from Mamie's kitchen. I realize this weekend has changed me, and deepened my resolve to learn everything I possibly can about food and my quest to become a professional chef.

My heart leaps when a fresh, new idea tickles my brain: I will learn special coastal recipes and bring them back for more kitchen experiences with Grandmother.

I will also collect amazing seashells as a gift for my dear Mamie. And when I return, together we will put them to our ears and listen to the ocean and maybe glean secrets about what lies ahead for the master chef and her assistant.

47

EIGHT

Summer Adventures
in Port-Vendres

I am convinced that children do not truly understand or experience the concept of freedom until they have been enrolled in school, struggled through a long winter of studying — and then summer arrives. Oh, what a sensation to realize you have ten free weeks of fun and sun stretching out before you.

That's the excitement I feel on June 22, 1979. I am so wound up Mom calls me "boisterous." It is not a compliment. I respond by saying my tall, fifteen-year-old brother Jean-Marc — three years my senior — is the boisterous one. And this sets off a little crisis.

My brother has butterflies in his stomach because in September I will start Grade 6 at the same school he attends, Sainte-Ursule, the Catholic high school in Pau. Naturally, it is run by nuns. But that's not why Jean-Marc is feeling anxious.

"I can't have you following me around, you know," he says.

"Why would I do that?"

"God he is dumb!"

I still don't get it, so I ask, "What's the problem?"

"Tell him! Will somebody tell him?"

Mother intervenes and suggests to Jean-Marc that it will be nice to have a family member so close.

"It's humiliating! A little kid sticking to me like glue!"

"I'm not a little kid!"

"Worse! You're a 'little' brother and you'll do silly things and embarrass me."

I'm more confused than ever because Jean-Marc and I are quite famous for doing silly things together at Pau Castle, on the public bus and in Mamie's kitchen.

"Just don't think you're invited to hang out with the older kids, because you're not," he says.

Our sister Christine observes our quarrel, but says nothing. She is the eldest, five years older than me, and wise for her years. Or maybe she's just relieved that she won't encounter me in her hallways because she attends Saint-Maur, a private girls-only school.

Mother finally attempts to calm the waters by reminding us that there is no point in fretting about autumn because summer vacation has just begun and there is much to do before the adventure begins.

Jean-Marc will not be consoled, so I say, "You're so boisterous."

✳✳✳

This week we are very busy because soon we'll be leaving for Port-Vendres, a fishing port on the Mediterranean coast near the Spanish border. Just as we do every summer, we'll spend a month at a big campground on a hillside, mere steps from the sea and the bustling harbor where fishing boats come and go.

But first we must prepare and meticulously check all the camping equipment — cots, sleeping bags, pillows, lamps, chairs, beach blankets, cookware — and ensure we have enough food staples such as salt, pepper, vinegar, oil, pasta, and sugar for

49

a family of five. We're actually a family of six, but my eldest brother Alain, who is nine years older than me, lives in Strasbourg, Alsace where he is a career airman. For some reason the air force won't let him take off for a month so he can fool around with his brothers and sister.

A week before we depart for Port-Vendres, the weather is good so we travel with the tent to the municipal camping grounds in Aramits, a small Bearnese village, where we have some family. This little jaunt is an important summer ritual. We pitch the tent for a few days so that the musty canvas has a chance to air out. The process also allows us to confirm that the tent seams are still waterproof and we have all the pegs, poles and ropes we need to properly stake our shelter.

The whole family gets involved, and the intensity and anticipation are palpable. July is the best, most beautiful time of the year, so we are thrilled to begin our vacation. Life is so different at the beach. It is calmer and less regimented. Even my parents are able to relax.

At 4:30 a.m. on July 1 Dad wakes us. We are so excited about the trip that we have barely slept. Breakfast is ready and the trailer loaded. All we need is another hour to pack the Renault 6, which, fortunately, has a large trunk for our many pieces of luggage. Even so, Mom has filled every inch of space under the front seats with smaller bags.

We leave Pau at about 6:00 a.m., and spend the morning driving through the south western French cities of Tarbes, Lannemezan, Saint-Giron, Foix, Lavelanet, Rivesaltes, Perpignan and Argeles-sur-Mer. We stop a few times for bathroom breaks — and coffee breaks for the driver — and also to have a bite to eat. Along the way we sing, doze off and enjoy the beautiful scenery passing by, until, at last, we arrive in Port-Vendres in mid-afternoon.

Sitting on the back seat between my brother and my sister, a rush of adrenalin overtakes me as I recognize the post office, the beach bar, the store with its beautiful buoys, and the pier where we fish in the evening. Ah, Port-Vendres, city of games, beach, family fun and fishing trips!

When we get to the Peninsula campground, Mom and Dad go to the reception to pay for our stay. They know the owners well since we've been coming to Port-Vendres every July for eight years.

Once we get to our campsite, we are surrounded by happy, exuberant people,

50

many of whom we know from previous vacations. The conviviality and numerous greetings make our arrival feel like a homecoming.

We quickly unload the trailer and spread out the enormous bag containing the huge blue tent canvas and the many different tent pegs. It's a family-size tent with amenities: a spacious cooking area in back; three bedrooms stretching along the right side; a living/dining room on the left that can be transformed into a sheltered play room on rainy days; and a big entranceway that gives us lots of room to eat and play cards, all while protected from the sun and rain.

Under Dad's supervision, my family quickly turns into a team of engineers. We sort the pegs by type and size, just as we rehearsed in Aramits. Then we assemble the roof's frame, and loosely fasten the support poles. Next we spread the canvas across most of the structure and tie the numerous small cords from the canvas to the poles to keep everything secure. When we're finally ready to hoist the tent, we each grab a corner pole and fellow campers who have been watching our progress suddenly swarm the unattended poles and the roof frame to assist our effort. That's when Dad starts counting.

"Everybody ready? One! Two! Three — LIFT!"

My heart pounds with joy as I pull with all my strength and watch as the flat canvas rises like a blue phoenix, miraculously flapping and spreading its wings into the shape of a summer home. Voila! Quickly, we jam pegs into the earth so that the base is securely in place. And then we stretch long support cords from the tops of posts to the ground so that the walls and roof remain taut and protective. Zany with glee, we slap each other's backs, generous in our thanks and praise. Summer vacation has begun!

We devote the rest of the afternoon to emptying the trailer and car. We fix up the tent quite nicely with our belongings as my parents meet with seasonal acquaintances, people like us who come to this rustic setting every year to replenish and refresh the soul. Soon the adults gather for an aperitif, everyone bringing their own glasses, bottles and snacks to nibble.

Fortunately, the sun has not set, so Christine, Jean-Marc and I make a run for the beach along the Mediterranean Sea where we'll engage in our vacation traditions: Swimming, of course, with lots of splashing and playing in the surf; sun bathing as we catch our breath before diving back into the water; and feeding our faces. Yes, eating lots of tasty treats is an essential part of beach life when our young bodies become ravished with hunger.

Our favorite treat is chichis. Whenever we go to the beach we know we'll buy the long pieces of fried dough resembling sticks that are sometimes braided for more thickness. This style of donut is also made in nearby Spain where they are called churros and often dunked in chocolate. Oh, how I love my chichis.

But I also have a favorite vender, so as soon as we arrive at the beach, I began looking for a caravan called Chichi Chez Marcel — and there it is. I run to greet Mr. Marcel, who recognizes me and gives me a piece of broken chichi that he cannot sell.

Mr. Marcel's chichis are the best on the planet. I say this with absolute confidence, though I have yet to travel much beyond the borders of France. They are about forty centimeters in length, equal to my outstretched arm, and three centimeters thick. Generously sprinkled with sugar and deep-fried to a beautiful golden hue, the dessert also comes with the seductive scent of cinnamon. Oh my goodness, the cruelty, and the injustice we vacationers suffer when the wind shifts and carries the tantalizing fragrance of the chichis toward the beach where we are baking in the sun.

On this particular day I chat with Mr. Marcel and tell him about the thrill of seeing our family tent rise again and how wonderful it is to know we'll be spending the entire month in Port-Vendres. He smiles, while helping other hungry beachcombers, and I am reminded that the amazing food I enjoy almost always includes one basic ingredient — warm, wonderful people who reward me with patience, laughter and good care.

When Christine, Jean-Marc and I finish our delicious treat, we return to the shoreline. The water is clear and warm and the beach is not very crowded. This will change in the next few days as the July vacationers arrive en masse. We alternate between bathing in the sea and bathing in the sun, and could not be happier.

As the day begins to fade my brother and sister and I — each with a chichi in hand — calmly return to the campground where a light dinner of salad and sandwiches is waiting. As we devour the food, we discuss with Dad whether we should go fishing on the pier this evening. Soon we admit we are all very tired from our exciting first day of summer vacation. We agree to go later in the week.

52

The days pass and our activities alternate between playing games at the campground and swimming at the beach. Many mornings, Jean-Marc and I wake up early to greet the fishing boats. By 8 a.m., we see the vessels coming in from the open sea and know their holds are full of fish.

At the harbor, we sit on rusty, salt-worn 100-year-old bollards and watch the fishermen maneuver and moor. Sometimes they let us help them unload the fish for auction. There are tons of fish of all types and sizes, but the most abundant is the sardine. Cases and cases of sardines must be brought to market.

Although Mom doesn't like it when we help the fishermen because we stink afterwards, it is so much fun! Often, even when we don't actually help them haul their catch, the fishermen give Jean-Marc and me a five-kilo case of sardines each. It is a true treasure because we know we will be able to sell them quickly at the campground and make a dandy sum of pocket money.

As we haul the sardines back to our tent, my brother and I negotiate the price per kilo we will charge and the quantity we will keep for our own consumption. Jean-Marc wants to sell our entire bounty, whereas I want to eat some. We agree to save three kilos for our family and I rush to leave them with Mom. Then I rejoin my big-brother business partner and we wander through the campsites, calling like fishmongers.

"Fresh sardines! Just caught!

"Get 'em cheap! Ten francs a kilo!"

Most of the campers know us, so we sell our sardines quickly and feel rich, netting thirty-five francs each. Doing this twice a week brings us both about seventy francs, equal to about forty dollars in 2013. Not bad for a twelve-year-old kid selling fish.

I enjoy the money and yet also know that the profitable experience with the sardines is a matter of survival. Early in life I learned to fend for myself without the expectation that my parents would or could fill my pockets with loose change. Little did I know that in the process of providing for my own basic needs I was also learning business skills that I would develop further throughout my adolescent years.

But at this age there is really only one thing on my mind. More summer fun in Port-Vendres!

53

NINE

Night Fishing on the Quay

Dad, Jean-Marc and I are fishing at the end of the deserted port quay that welcomes vessels from the Mediterranean Sea. We walked the extra distance to our special spot where there are no bright street lamps or public utilities. Most of the fishing boats have left in search of a big catch and the night is clear and beautiful under a full moon. I enjoy the quiet and calm that darkness brings. The throbbing noise of daily life is replaced by the soft, drifting music of voices engaged in relaxed conversation. The sea breezes are soothing, too.

"I wish the full moon came out every night," I say.

Jean-Marc snorts, of course. "That's so stupid."

Dad smiles and says, "That's a nice thought, Eric. We can wish, can't we?"

The quay hangs over the lapping water, so all we need to do is lay fishing poles down on the surface and let our lines dangle over the edge and into the sea. To attract fish we illuminate the sea bed with powerful electric torches that have been lowered beneath our hooks and bait.

Thanks to Mamie — yes, Grandma is also a shrewd, skilled fisherwoman — we are very serious about our fishing expeditions. The hooks we're using are a bit bigger than those we would choose for river fishing, and the lure is quite different, too. Selecting the correct hooks and lures is essential to our success, of course, because fish, like people, have personalities and are attracted to different types of shapes, movements and colors. For example, you must avoid chrome-plated hooks for sea bream and select short-stemmed upside-down hooks for sea bass and sea bream.

The bait must also be chosen with care. In Bearn, we usually fish with maggots, earthworms or caddis worms. In Port-Vendres, we use bread and bits of cheese.

We don't have to wait long before we see a tug on our lines. We haul up a few sea breams, mullets and other kinds of fish, but throw most of them back into the sea for various reasons. The sea bream, for example, would make a fairly good meal, if not for all the bones it contains. Whereas the mullet doesn't have much flavor, tastes a bit salty, and also has lots of bone to pick through. Even so, we keep the latter because it provides good bait when we use a crayfish net for capturing our dinner.

Just like the other fishermen who are spread out at irregular intervals along the quay, we're patient because we know it is wise to be picky. The breams are a much better meal; especially the royal gilt-head bream, recognizable by the yellow ring on its nose. The sea bass, otherwise known as loup de mer in the Mediterranean Sea and bar in the Atlantic Ocean, is also delicious. Connoisseurs refer to these schools of fish as "noble" and they are much sought after but not easily hooked. They are crafty and quick, and when they finally take the bait they resist and struggle so fiercely that they commonly succeed in unhooking themselves and escaping.

Dad, Jean-Marc and I are excited when we spot a couple of gilt head breams investigating the commotion caused by the mullets and sea breams that foolishly attack our lures. We move our fishing lines closer to the approaching breams, and this turns out to be a smart move because the sea breams seem nervous about the encroaching nobles and quickly disappear into the dark reaches of the sea. Now we can give our full attention to the breams that circle, sniff and eyeball the lures, but do not bite. I can feel myself grow tense and know Dad and Jean-Marc also are on edge. We are hungry for our first summer vacation haul, our taste buds and nostrils flare with the memory of delicate fish steaming on the outdoor grill. Then suddenly our visitors turn and swim away.

The disappointment is huge. It is as though the full moon has collapsed and every twinkling star has burned out. We decide to change our lures with fresher bait, and do so with speed. Miraculously, the gilt-head breams return immediately after our lures break the surface of the water and plunge the depths. We pray for a feeding frenzy, but once again the royal fish touch without biting, linger for a few minutes, and then move into the shadows, only to return a couple times to taunt us. Smart fish. They must know we want to invite them to dinner.

Hours pass on the quay; we talk, laugh, two sons and a very good father on summer vacation. In a flash I experience a revelatory moment: if some greater being is watching from outer space it may very well be witnessing a long string of bright lights — orbs of happy fisherman — strung out along our wharf, happy to be waiting for the chance to hook the sea's bounty.

Suddenly, out of nowhere, a gorgeous sea bass pitches itself open-mouthed at my lure and then attempts to continue on its way, until I manage to snag it. When the fish feels the sting of the hook, it attempts to flee, and I would too if suddenly I felt something sharp rip a hole in my lip. We begin to fight, a boy and a dream catch. It is a beautiful battle. I lean backwards as my fishing pole bends dramatically under the power of the brave, desperate bass. The electricity of mighty foes meeting in the Port-Vendres black night burns my hands as my pole transmits every jerk, vibrant angle and agile run toward freedom.

Dad and Jean-Marc rush to my side to give me plenty of advice.

"Let it go, give it a bit of line, son!" Dad says.

Moments later, my big brother shouts, "Enough! Enough! Get it back!"

"Slowly," my wise father whispers.

I feel like an Olympian, a French god, and yet I am a mere pre-adolescent who is standing shoulder to shoulder with family giants and practicing the ancient ritual of harvesting the Earth's bounty.

The fish thrashes about like the Devil and then, exhausted from the struggle with fate, offers mild resistance. My sea bass knows it has met its match, and I know I have survived the challenge as I drag in my magnificent catch.

But not so fast, Eric. When Jean-Marc reaches out with the landing net, the sea bass suddenly regains its strength and begins another intense battle. If I don't give it some slack, the thrashing fish may break my line and disappear into the dark sea. I slowly let it out and know everything is back to square one. Boy against fish. With more guidance from Dad and Jean-Marc, I continue my angling and wrangling — with aching arms — and it all feels like a struggle without mercy where anything could happen.

Fortunately, the outburst that nearly ruined my big fish story has a happy ending when the great sea bass surrenders, exhausted, and is scooped into the landing net. Victory at last! We shout and jump with joy because we all have had a hand in capturing the fish. Without my team, I know I would not have succeeded.

✳✳✳

We decide to call it a night, but, before leaving, we lower a trap into the water at the end of the quay. From the outside, it looks like a simple six-foot-long cylindrical net with wide round openings at each end. In truth, each opening narrows like a funnel. The fish quickly swim through the spacious entryways in search of food that is placed in the mid-section of the net. Only then do the sea creatures realize it is impossible to swim back out.

We place pieces of mullet and a chicken carcass left over from lunch in the net and then throw it into the sea. The long cord attached to our trap is fastened to a rock along the quay. We leave with the hope that we'll catch something. Maybe tomorrow we'll find a crab or, even better, a lobster or conger eel. If not, we'll just add more pieces of bread and meat scraps and reposition everything for another day. After all, it is summer and we have plenty of time.

At dinner time the next day, Dad washes the fish we caught and lights the barbecue; flames shoot upward and then disappear as the coals begin to heat up and burn evenly. Next, Dad seasons our catch with salt, black pepper, and a trickle of olive oil and then lays my sea bass — our biggest fish — on the sizzling grill. Soon he adds the sea breams. He turns the fish over, and then lightly covers them in more olive oil. The barbecue spews smoke and the strong scent of fish spreads throughout the campground. I observe Dad checking the

57

food to make sure it is properly cooked, and then I help him transfer our prize to an absolutely horrible, cheap plastic serving tray. Hey, this isn't a four-star restaurant, we are camping! We enjoy the fish with salad and the whole family relishes the meal because it is so fresh and delicious.

While we continue eating, Dad lays the sardines Jean-Marc and I procured in a special tool he has devised for grilling. The two racks look like stiff, charred slices of bread — a large metal sandwich — and hold can numerous small fish so that they will cook very slowly. This technique also allows the rows of sardines to be flipped in unison without mishap. Brilliant. My dad is a genius. When the little ones are ready to eat we sprinkle them with a mixture of melted butter, sautéed shallots, garlic, parsley, chives and lemon juice. Heaven!

As we savor the flavors of grilled seafood, we take turns sharing the exploits of our fishing expedition and discuss what might have happened if the breams had taken our bait. But, alas, they are very cunning fish compared to the voracious sea bass that unwarily swallowed my lure.

In the days that follow, Dad, Jean-Marc and I regularly check the trap we set after our first night of fishing. No luck, at first. Yet during one of our inspections, the trap seems to be stuck on some rocks at the bottom of the port, and it appears that some seaweed is tangled in the net. We figure the current probably moved its position overnight, so we decide to pull it up and place it elsewhere. But it is stubborn and won't easily rise to the surface of the water. As we double our effort we are overcome with a keen suspicion that something is inside our fishing net.

As our trap flops onto the pier we are stunned to encounter the sharp fangs and angry hissing of a conger eel. The sea creature opens its mouth, bares its dangerous teeth and lunges at us, ready and willing to fight for its life.

"Stand back, boys!"

We don't argue with Dad because at first Jean-Marc and I are scared silly by this fearless marine monster. The eel is huge and lively, and we are not equipped to do battle. But our shouts and excitement are loud enough to alert a few nearby fishermen who rush to our rescue and sever the eel's head with a cleaver.

Still and glistening in the sun, the conger is a beautiful specimen. We estimate its weight at approximately ten kilos, while its length nearly matches my height of about five feet. Even the fishermen have to admit that our lucky

CHAPTER NINE

catch is gorgeous.

At dinner time Jean-Marc teases me about our adventure with the eel.

"Mom, you should have heard him squeal! Like a little piglet."

This time I don't have to defend myself. Dad is quick to remind my big brother that he too made some funny noises and hopped around when the conger showed its long fangs.

"But we give thanks to the sea for bringing us such a fine catch. And let's not forget to thank Mamie for teaching us how to fish, eh, boys?" Dad says.

"That calls for a toast," Jean-Marc says. "Wine anyone?"

"Flat water for you, wise guy," Mom says, and we all laugh.

Not that Mom was so amused when we proudly arrived with the conger earlier in the day. Even without its head, the eel's body continued to writhe and wriggle in the bucket where we stashed it. She refused to cook it until the involuntary spasms, which lasted all day, finally stopped. Our Mediterranean monster scared her even though she never saw its dagger-like teeth.

To prepare the meal Dad slices the long creature into sections that are about 1.5 inches thick. Then he seasons, flours and sautés the eel in olive oil with white wine and a Herbes de Provence mixture, which typically includes savory, fennel, basil and thyme. I am shocked because I thought the herbs were only appropriate for use when grilling lamb and other meats. Even while camping I am learning so much about creativity in the kitchen.

Prepared Provencal style, and served with slices of tomato, onion and garlic, our tempestuous eel turns out to be quite a delicious dish.

TEN

Escape to Catalonia

The sun is already heating up despite the early morning hour. We are driving toward the Costa Brava coast, heading to Figueres in Catalonia, Spain for a stroll and to buy a few things, specifically wine, Ricard, Port and other aperitifs.

After leaving Port-Vendres, we stop in Banyuls-sur-Mer where we often go to stroll on the seafront in the evening. The area is dotted with terraces, cafés and restaurants where we stop for ice cream while the adults drink sangria. The region grows wine grapes and we cross many Banyuls vineyards that have the appellation d'origine contrôlée, or AOC, the official certification that guarantees the quality of French produce, especially wines and cheeses. The wine from this region is smooth and natural, made from old vines grown on terraces along the rugged Pyrénées hillsides that hang over the Mediterranean.

In Banyuls-sur-Mer, we continue our walk and the sites are magnificent: The sea is a beautiful, brilliant turquoise blue. It is market day and we buy fruit, cookies and cold drinks for a seaside picnic. We spend a few hours near an inlet on a small beach that is gravelly; the tiny stones are soft under our feet. The sea is calm and warm and Mom finds a bit of shade under a stone pine tree twisted by the wind. She sets up a makeshift camp with one area for eating and another for resting and napping.

We continue on our journey in the early afternoon, driving alongside the sea and eventually crossing the border as we head towards Llançà to enjoy the view and ocean air. Before long, the Spanish countryside turns into a genuine oven. All the car windows are down and the hot wind blows on our faces. Everyone complains about the heat but I am enjoying it: I feel as though I am being baked like a potato by its purity.

Eventually, we arrive at our final destination. Figueres is a city full of treasures. We find the Saint-Père church district with its big tower, the San Fernando Castle with its magnificent fortress built to ward off the constant attacks by the French. And then there is the Dali museum-theater, named for the master with the pointy mustache who was born in this city.

Figueres is also a city of fragrances and aromas, thanks to its markets and bars serving tapas all day long, and a city of celebrations which end late in the night. All these charms combined make this an exceptional place.

We stop for an hour to visit the castle with its old stone tunnels where we cool off a bit. After the castle we go to the Dali museum. Facing the entrance we are struck by the extravagant and eccentric architecture of the museum so befitting to the artist. We are stunned by the building's tall walls and tower, all colored in the shade of blood red. The man was greedy and had a very good eye, proof of which can be seen in one section of the museum and on the tower, both of which are decorated with golden statues and sumptuous giant eggs. To visit this museum is to visit a parallel world, an imaginary and eccentric place quite bizarre and batty. We take it all in and also appreciate the cool vibe of the exhibition rooms.

Thirsty and starting to feel quite hungry, we leave the museum and head to a tapas bar on a nearby street corner. Speaking Spanish, Dad orders drinks and tapas to munch on because later we will be eating paella. Can't wait!

Everyone orders a bottle of cold milk chocolate except Dad who has a beer. A small dish of marinated olives is brought to the table. These are regional olives, pickled and then marinated by the proprietress with lots of spices, peeled red peppers and lemon slices. Later, the proprietress returns with a dish in each hand and a big smile. On our wooden table she places a small bowl of lightly grilled almonds, spiced with mild smoked paprika, and an oval dish with a dozen mussels on the half shell stuffed with parsley, garlic and bread crumbs. Her husband assists her by bringing out more tapas, which include a beautiful Spanish omelet, called tortilla, cut in triangles, a small dish of chicken nuggets in a Romesco sauce and a few button mushrooms sautéed a la plancha. Everyone is delighted. Like natives, we partake in tapeo, the act of going out to eat tapas. But the custom usually means visiting several bars within a few hours. We're quite happy to stay where we are.

The slightly spiced almonds are appetizing and crunchy, and they make our mouths water. The omelet is succulent with the wholesome flavors of potatoes and fresh eggs that are blessed with rich, high-grade yokes. We eat the mussels right from the shell and the mixture of mussels and bread crumbs saturated with garlic butter is absolutely delicious. The chicken nuggets are shaped like fat fingers. When dunked in a mildly spicy sauce made with tomatoes and almonds, I am surprised and pleased with bursts of tang.

Fully satisfied, we slowly walk back along streets full of shoppers. Here we find a hat, there a few bottles of wine and spirits. But not too much since we must go through customs on our way back to our camp.

It is 8:00 p.m. when we head for a restaurant more than ready for dinner. We're disappointed when the waitress tells us that they won't begin to serve for another hour. Nine o'clock is nearly our bedtime. Spain likes to eat late.

When Mom protests and says she doesn't want to wait another hour for dinner, Dad gamely negotiates with the chef, who eventually agrees to serve us early. Tourists! We sit down and order paella for four knowing full well that there will be enough for five since the waitress has warned us that the dish is generous. Bring it on!

A group of men sitting in the back of the restaurant playing cards cast an annoyed glance our way. They are unhappy, apparently, that the chef must leave their game so that he can prepare our meal.

Thirty minutes later, the waitress clears the center of our table and then returns with a large flat-bottom pan, gripping it by the handles with two white dishtowels so as not to burn herself. The pan is big enough to cook and serve the paella according to a long, unaltered Spanish tradition. It is an abundant dish of saffron steamy rice, peas, pieces of chicken, calamari, mussels, big shrimp and other seafood. The superb paella has arrived!

The waitress serves us each a huge portion of the aromatic concoction and once again I experience the sensation of being royalty. Ever since Mamie fed us her glorious a poule au pot whenever we eat fine dishes I like to say that we are eating a meal "made for a king." The paella is excellent.

When the chef comes to our table to make sure everything is all right, Dad generously compliments him, telling him the food lives up to his reputation as mentioned by the proprietress of the tapas bar. I pay close attention to the conversation. Even if I don't understand what the chef is saying in Spanish, I admire his ability to bring so much pleasure to people by branding their taste buds with an unforgettable culinary experience.

Following our superb dinner, we head back to where our car is parked. Earlier in the day the streets were crowded with people, mainly tourists. But now the streets are positively jam-packed and chaotic. We'll soon learn that the excess traffic is caused by locals who have finished work and are ready for some fun. We hold hands tightly so as not to be swept away as a few cars slowly attempt to make their way through the throng. When we are finally in the car we joke that we have more space in our little Renault 6 than we had walking in the streets of Figueres.

The joking stops when Dad tries unsuccessfully to drive through the swarms of loud, rollicking people. We are confused that our hosts seem so angry with us; they yell insults and willfully block our passage. When we come upon an intersection blocked by police, Dad asks for directions and learns that for a couple days motorized traffic isn't allowed from 6 p.m. to 5 a.m. due to a popular local celebration. Fortunately, the police officer realizes we are tourists and suggests a short-cut to get us out of the area. But this too confounds Dad. He carefully repeats the policeman's directions several times: turn right at the first one-way street, keep straight and then turn right again at a second one-way street — against the flow of human traffic.

"Are you sure?" Dad asks.

"Yes, that's right. If anyone complains tell them a policeman gave you permission to go this way."

Empowered with this information, we carefully drive through the crowds of raucous, vocal people, all the while yelling out our open windows, "The cop told us to go this way!" Finally, we reach the road heading back to our campground and sit back in our seats with a sigh of relief. Tourists!

∗∗∗

The next morning is declared a beach and nap day. It is hard to believe that this is one of our last summer vacation days before we must head back home. I reflect upon our adventures and realize Port-Vendres is truly amazing. Like so many other years, we've had a fabulous time while meeting people from all over France and Europe. As I stroll to the sea, I look at the license plates on the cars that dot the campground and realize they are all quite revealing and unique, just like the accents, gestures and personalities of the wonderful people who surround us.

I also ponder the excellent Spanish chef, Mamie and my Aunt Jeannette who all succeed so well pleasing others through their artistry in the kitchen. There was a time, I admit, when like many boys my age I had wanted to be a fireman. But that phase disappeared because I am surrounded by people who have the magic touch. They understand and practice the tradition of raising the spirits with fine meals. Their gift reinforces my goal. I am all the more determined to follow in their footsteps and make food and hospitality my career.

As my culinary intentions and tasting adventures continue, my desire to be a chef grows. I see myself in a chef's hat and apron and naively believe this will be impressive when flirting with girls — not that I am quite ready for that kind of excitement yet.

CHAPTER TEN

ELEVEN

Barbecue at The Morins

Mom's health is frail and the early months of 1980 have been difficult for her and the whole family. She spent several weeks in a clinic and when she came home it was decided that we will not go to Port-Vendres for summer vacation this year. Instead, we will spend the time with our friends, Jean-Claude and Claudine Morin and their daughter Emmanuelle. This arrangement will give Mom a chance to rest, but it will be a bit hectic for Dad: he'll stay with us on the weekends and return to Pau during the work week.

We met the Morins years ago at the campground in Port-Vendres. I was four or five years old at the time and often visited their caravan to play with their dog Sarah. This is how we all became such fast friends; my parents would search for me and always find me with the Morins. Now we regularly vacation at their home, and have watched Emmanuelle grow from infancy.

Jean-Claude is an industrialist whose company manufactures trucks. As far as I'm concerned, his factory, which is nearby, is a terrific playground. Before opening his factory, Jean-Claude worked for the French car manufacturer, Renault, where he designed the Renault 12, a popular model which sold 2.5 million units.

The Morins live in an old renovated farmhouse in the village of L'Echalusse in the Cher region of central France. Dad often works on the grounds during our stays, usually on the stone facades. The farmhouse is big and beautiful with large French windows and exposed ceiling beams. On one side of the house, the Morins transformed a ballroom into a play room; a basketball court was created outside. On the opposite side, Mr. Jacques, a neighbor and professional gardener, tends to a big vegetable garden. Claudine uses much of the produce for cooking and preserving.

The garden is well organized, with rows of tomatoes, peas and green beans on one side and, on the other side, all the hardy plants trained to grow up support sticks and ropes. The lettuce, herbs and carrots are laid out one after another, interspersed with many rows of small red fruit. The birds are very happy to peck away at the produce, even when the Morin's dog Sarah barks and runs toward them, in an attempt to chase them away. When she isn't rushing the garden, Sarah lies in wait at the corner of the terrace, growling to warn the airborne invaders that she is always watching. I love Sarah and wish she could live with us in Pau. But I know she would not be happy. She needs the great outdoors, and Mother would always be griping about keeping everything clean. That's why we were never allowed to have a pet of any kind.

One thing Sarah cannot do is keep the children out of the garden, and this exasperates poor Mr. Jacques, who is a perfectionist. While gardening he notices that his rubber shoes make holes in the soft soil. His solution is to attach rectangular planks to his soles so that the aisles between the vegetable rows appear neat and untouched — until a gaggle of wild, playful children sweep through his paradise.

Yes, we play all day long and can't help but get ourselves into all kinds of trouble every couple of hours. Punishment usually comes in the form of chores, and we are given no opportunity to appeal. Claudine excels in assigning chores, the worse probably being shucking peas. Sitting on a stool with a big bowl between our legs, we pod the peas one by one until the bowl is full. This tedious task consumes hours and we are always happy with the bigger pods because they will fill the bowl faster.

Even so, Jean-Marc tells me that I don't work fast enough.

"Why are you so slow?"

66

"I'm not slow, I'm careful."

"Careful with a peapod?"

Actually, I am transfixed by the beauty of the peas, their uniform size, nearly round, well aligned and connected to the pod by a mini stem. Their color is a vivid light green and I have a hard time imagining how the canned peas we eat at home once resembled these small jewels. From time to time, I pop a few raw peas into my mouth and savor the tender, sweet and delicious morsels.

Another chore is to remove the tops and tails of the string beans. Fortunately, this takes much less time because the beans are a lot bigger than peas and quickly fill the bowl. We simply break the ends off and pull away the seam that is like thread embedded along one side of each bean.

Despite all the work — food preparation, actually, and in hindsight part of my education — we are truly enjoying our vacation. While Mom relaxes the children freely run through the fields and play in Jean-Claude's nearby factory. We also often visit the Morin' extended family and friends in the area where we are always treated to delicious jam with the afternoon tea.

✳✳✳

This week everyone is very busy because on Saturday the Morins are having a big party featuring piglets roasted over an open pit. About eighty people are expected and it is Dad who will oversee the roasting because that was his assignment years ago in North Africa where he served as a soldier during the Algerian War.

Dad tells me that, in the traditional Algerian style, a sheep is roasted because Muslims don't eat pork. But to feed the number of guests invited to our event, we would have to cook several lambs. So a decision is made to roast two twelve-kilo piglets instead. That's about twenty-six pounds of meat.

Our days are devoted to preparation and running many errands, including the purchase of paper plates, glasses and napkins. Mom decides that she will prepare sangria similar to what we drink in Banyuls-sur-Mer (near Port-Vendres); she will also help make the salads. The desserts will be provided by the guests who have been asked to bring a pie or cake.

The Wednesday before the party, we start digging a pit for the fire at the end

67

of the garden near the garage. Dad builds a roasting rack using some rubble he has plastered together and four steel bars. The bars are notched in four places and will be used to raise and lower the pork during the cooking process.

Jean-Claude, ever the engineer, designed and forged the steel bars, as well as the roasting spits at his factory. The long spits have been dropped off at the village butcher shop where they will be inserted as the piglets are being prepared for the roast.

It takes a couple days to complete the roasting pit and, when it is done, we pack soil around the hole to prevent anyone from falling in. We haul wood logs from the storeroom, pile them up in rows along the low wall of the pit and then cover them with a tarpaulin in case of rain.

We spend Friday running last-minute errands, including a visit to the butcher. The Morin's place is only a few hundred meters from the village center, and so Jean-Claude, my Dad, Jean-Marc and I go there on foot in the afternoon as arranged with Mr. Patrice, the butcher.

When we arrive, he is cleaning a sirloin at his butcher's block next to the customer counter. Such stabbing and hacking! Slabs of fat fall with each vigorous cut, and the butcher looks up and welcomes us with a hearty voice.

"Hi, sirs. You came with reinforcements!"

Jean-Claude replies, "The pig is man's work. So here we all are."

"A drove of pigs, young and old."

Our host feigns insult. "Not so old, Mr. Patrice. And my friends from Pau have come all this way to be called pigs?"

"Pigs from Pau!" Jean-Marc chimes in, and everyone laughs.

More jovial exchanges follow, and then Mr. Patrice gets down to business. He explains that the piglets will be ready soon.

"I've stuffed them. They will be delicious. My assistant is just now sewing them up."

"May we watch?" Jean-Claude asks.

"Yes, yes," the butcher replies. "But please don't frighten my assistant. He prefers pigs that don't ask questions."

More laughter. And I am reminded how much fun food can be. It raises the spirits. I am evermore certain that I will make a life in the kitchen.

When we move to the back of the shop we see our two piglets laid out on a big table where the assistant is stitching them along the gut with a trussing needle and steel thread. The durable materials will keep the stuffing — a delicious mixture of ground pork, garlic, onions, herbs, dried apples and walnuts — inside the animal during the long roast. Whole pigs that have been butchered look pale and naked; the sight is not particularly appetizing, especially since their eyes have been removed.

As we watch, the butcher gives us some cooking tips. He believes our pigs may need ten or so hours to roast, because they must be placed far from the flames. "And they should be turned over and constantly basted with marinade."

We return home both reassured and a bit worried. Reassured because the pigs are gorgeous and the butcher has agreed to deliver them tomorrow at nine sharp. But worried and a bit anxious because we'll have to start the fire at around six o'clock in the morning, which is a lot earlier than we had planned.

That evening, we all gather around the Morin's huge kitchen table which can seat a dozen people. The ambiance is joyful, the aperitifs flow freely and the menu is light and easy — homemade croque-monsieur with salad and fruit from the garden. The croques are mellow, crunchy and perfectly grilled, and the rich Swiss cheese melts in my mouth. The sandwich is nicely complemented by slices of white ham and light, buttery bread. Everyone enjoys the dinner, and after cleaning up we all turn in because tomorrow will be a long, rigorous day.

✳✳✳

I wake up at eight o'clock, kiss everyone good morning and go to meet up with the men at the roasting pit.

Dad and Jean-Claude have already started the fire which crackles angrily. The flames, high and furious, have begun to devour, as fast as possible, the

69

twenty or so logs that lay in the pit. The idea is to let the flames burn down as they transform the wood into a good thick layer of embers. Only then can we properly position the pigs, ideally over flames that cannot reach up to lick and burn their skins — at least a meter below the pork. The meat will be tender and delicious if it is roasted slowly, ever so slowly, and basted regularly with marinade. I can hardly wait.

Our marinade — a mix of white wine, oil and herbs — was prepared yesterday and is ready to be poured into the pail that has been placed by the pit. Beside the pail rests our marinade brush, a broomstick with a balled-up cloth that has been attached on one end with wire and nails.

Mr. Patrice arrives in his truck and backs into the courtyard. After inspecting the fire he suggests we spread out the burning logs a bit to reduce the height of the pile they create. Then the stuffed piglets, speared on the spits, are unloaded from the vehicle and laid onto the rack over the fire and set at the highest height the four notches will allow.

Jean-Claude has invented an ingenious system that will allow us to simultaneously rotate the piglets. On each side of the pigs' heads a pulley-type steel disk has been inserted. The disks are connected to a chain which, in turn, is linked to a wheel placed on the side of the roasting rack. When the wheel is turned, both pigs will spin in a rotisserie-style motion. The engineer is very proud of himself. And I am impressed with his clever mechanical mind.

Every hour, the men take turns rotating the pigs, basting them with marinade, feeding the fire and managing the height of the flames. Of course, Jean-Marc and I choose to spend most of the day near the fire tending to the barbecue. By mid-afternoon the pigs are really starting to cook. We watch the melting fat escape in droplets that sizzle and set off short-lived blazes when they fall onto the embers.

Although by now the flames have been profoundly reduced, the ember bed is so thick that an intense, steady heat continues to emanate upward. Also, the marinade has now had hours to seep through the pork, which has created a wholesome and tantalizing aroma that fills the surrounding air. Many neighbors, attracted by the rich smell, come to greet us throughout the day. They have, of course, been invited to tonight's feast, and I can tell that, like me, they can barely wait to taste this tender, juicy meat.

70

Toward the end of the afternoon, we place long table tops on trestles in a continuous row under the fruit trees in an orchard near the garden. We cover the surface with a big roll of white paper. Armed with a huge stapler from Jean-Claude's factory, my sister Christine tacks down the covering at regular intervals to create a tablecloth. We don't want the paper to blow away should the wind pick up.

A bar and the buffet table have already been set up in a nearby clearing. The bar is stocked with a pile of plastic glasses and three heavy wooden stands for wine barrels; one each for red, white and rosé wine. For now, the barrel of red wine is in the basement of the farm house, while the barrels of white and rosé are in the refrigerated butcher truck that Mr. Patrice kindly left behind this morning to keep drinks and salads cold.

The Morins summer roast festival is officially underway when we enlist the first guests that arrive to help us carry the wine barrels to the serving area. Mother's big container of sangria, which has been marinating since the night before, is brought to the table where it will be served as an aperitif.

Now the parade of sumptuous food dishes begins. Lumpfish egg hors d'oeuvres compete with mini-skewers of grilled marinated vegetables, cheese-filled puff pastry sticks, and bowls of chips, peanuts, almonds and other nibbles. In less than an hour, the front expanse of the Morins property is nearly overflowing with cars, as most of the guests have arrived.

Jean-Marc and I take it upon ourselves to act as the official greeters. As guests enter the farm grounds, we say, "Five francs, please. Yes, that's five per person, sir. Such a deal!"

Some neighbors smile and ignore us, while others haggle over price in a friendly, spirited sort of way; but most just hand over some loose change. Astounding! What a lesson for a couple young entrepreneurs — just ask. After all, we had to do something to create a revenue stream. This summer we don't have sardines to hawk.

Following an aperitif, most guests stroll to the fire pit and pay their respects to the roasting pigs; they admire the rich color and the supremely pleasing aroma. The marinade pail is almost empty and Dad is rotating the pork more often: he doesn't want any portion to overcook.

71

By eight o'clock the fire is dying, the flames are gone and all that remains of the logs and embers is a thick blanket of white ash. The main course has been roasting since late morning and it is nearly ready.

At dusk on this beautiful August day the adults are first to storm the buffet that is covered with salads and appetizers. They reach for basil and tomato salad, cucumber with cream and chives, and grated carrots with oranges and grapes from Corinth. They also fill their plates with slices of various quiches and meat terrines. When the children are allowed to begin, I load big spoonfuls of food on my plate and grab for a handful of chips. The ambiance is merry and the music so catchy that the meal is interrupted when some guests spontaneously begin to dancing along the terrace of the main house.

At last, the piglets are removed from the fire pit and brought to a table that has been covered with aluminum foil and large cutting boards. Mr. Patrice has been given the honor of cutting the meat, and he has brought his big knives. The one he has nicknamed "the hacker" has a large blade that is slightly bent at the tip. It looks really strange to me, but it is a true professional butcher's knife. Not even Mamie owns such a unique tool.

Guests gather around the carving area squealing with admiration for the beautiful, perfectly golden pigs.

"Ooo la-la!" says one woman.

Another lady cannot find the words and so merely gushes as she claps her hands together. "Oh!" I fear she might faint.

A man asks, "How long have they been roasting?"

"The pigs or my friend from Pau?"

Dad smiles because, as always, he has done the lion's share of work, slathering the piglets with marinade and raking the embers to create an even heat. His brow drips with perspiration.

The guests praise Dad and Jean-Claude for their excellent management of the roast, and then with mouths watering and eyes closed they inhale the delectable aroma. Feeling triumphant or merely overjoyed with the summer spectacle, one man blissfully sings the opening refrain of "La Marseillaise," the French National Anthem.

CHAPTER ELEVEN

"Let's get some pictures!" The woman with a small camera in her hand guides the master roasters to stand close to the pit and piglets.

"And let's get the children, too."

"Yes, before we roast them later," Jean-Claude jokes.

We swarm the mighty men and make silly faces and change our positions as we hear the camera click, again and again.

Mr. Patrice, meanwhile, carves piping-hot, steaming pieces of pork and places them on big platters that are delivered to the long table in the orchard. Hungry men, women and children waste no time devouring their food as more plates arrive generously stacked with meat that smells of wood and deeply embedded marinade.

Each diner is offered to pork, portions of the stuffing, and the skin which is golden, crunchy and delicious. We all have our favorite ways of enjoying the pork. We choose from condiments such as Dijon mustard, old-fashioned Meaux mustard, cornichons (small pickled gherkins), marinated onions, as well as tomato and onion conserve. Actually, most people take a sample of everything so as to savor a wide array of flavors.

After the main course, guests wander under a starry sky between the garden, the ballroom and the terrace, helping themselves to more food and beverages. Many retreat indoors when the evening air turns chilly.

When the dessert buffet is set up in the garden, the ballroom quickly empties. The entire human race always seems greedy for sweet treats. Not that I can blame anyone. Each guest has contributed a baked masterpiece, simple or complex, making the dessert selection deliriously impressive. Despite the lavish choices, I quickly spot cakes that make me swoon and, as it turns out, I am one of the first to serve myself. I help myself to a small slice of an apricot and pistachio tart, a small strawberry tart, a slice of quatre-quart cake and a handful of cherries. And this is only the start!

The party goes late into the night. Who would want such a feast to end? Yet all good things must pass, and so slowly the merriment fades and party guests drift to their cars and disappear down the country road, red tail lights gleaming in the shadow of midnight.

CHAPTER ELEVEN

As I watch the crowd dwindle, I realize this wonderful summer is also coming to an end. We will leave L'Echalusse in mid-August, only a couple of weeks away. I've had a thoroughly enjoyable time shouting, carousing, laughing, eating — and getting into a lot of trouble. And so it would seem, even to me, the prankster, that maybe it is time to grow up.

The realization brings some tension to the pit of my stomach. I am eagerly looking forward to learning the ropes of the cooking profession, but I still have two more school grades to complete before the great adventure will officially begin.

Oh well. The wait means I still have a little time left in my childhood. I sigh and tell myself, Enjoy.

TWELVE

English Lessons and the Parish Priest's Omelet

I am now in 6th grade and the school year is difficult. I am struggling to keep up with my classmates. My real weakness is languages, especially English. So I should not be surprised that my English teacher Miss Bellock hates me. She is a wicked and sadistic woman. When returning corrected tests during class she regularly saves mine for last. This technique allows her to humiliate me in front of the other students.

"And as always, the most hopeless test is kept for last. Mr. Arrouzé, six over twenty, and one point was awarded for the ink you used. I'll speak to your parents and request that you be sent to me for private tutoring on Wednesday afternoons. You must study more seriously, Mr. Arrouzé, if you expect to get anywhere in life."

I am crimson with shame, and wonder why she always saves me until the end and comments aloud. Why me when I know a handful of other pupils have grades inferior to mine? There is no way I will spend my Wednesday afternoons at her home instead of visiting Mamie or visiting the town library.

"I won't do it."

"Yes, you will," Dad says after a phone call from the Wicked Witch of Pau.

"I won't!"

"I work hard to send you to a good school. I do it so you won't have to break your back lifting stone and working on Sundays to support a family. You'll go!"

Weeks pass as I continue my stubborn protest. Yet before the Christmas holidays, I find myself attending private lessons at the home of the wretched Miss Bellock. I join several other pupils at her doorstep that first afternoon. As we chat, I realize they detest her every bit as much as I do.

A few weeks later, it appears that I am making progress and yet my marks are not improving. Miss Bellock uses this conundrum to persuade my parents that it might be best to send me to England where a host family will take me in and help me improve my English. Mom and Dad seem to approve of the concept, which surprises me since it will be rather costly and require my parents to make still more financial sacrifices on my behalf. Just like the private lessons, I initially protest my teacher's suggestion. But the truth is the idea of going abroad without my family excites me. I secretly vow to find new ways to make money so that I can contribute to the cost of travel with my own savings.

✳✳✳

A healthy portion of my pocket money comes from helping the priest serve Mass in the neighborhood parish. Jean-Marc and I have been altar boys for approximately two years; we assist every Sunday morning, as well as most Saturday wedding ceremonies and baptisms. In other words, we know the religious hymns like the back of our hands, and occasionally sing too loudly, which elicits a subtle kick behind the alter from the parish priest, his signal that we must lower our voices.

The priest is not the only one who wishes we'd blend into the choir. On Sunday, always at the nine o'clock Mass, a frail elderly lady sits in the front pew and sings at the top of her lungs. She is normally sweet, but constantly scolds us after the ritual for overpowering her singing, which annoys her tremendously.

We take the lectures in stride because we love serving Mass. It's our cash cow, as there is always a collection basket labeled "for altar boys" that enriches us. Frequently, after a baptism or a wedding, I make a lot of money, often several hundred francs. I enter the church with poor pockets but exit wealthy.

On the way home I stop at the newspaper stand and buy the journal for Dad, a football magazine for Jean-Marc, Christine magazine for my sister with the same name, flowers for Mom and a big cake for the family that I personally choose at the pastry shop. After the gifts have been delivered, I put on my poker face, shrug and say, "I spent all my money."

Of course, this is a ruse. I have already hid what's left of my bounty under my foot, inside my sock, because I am certain my parents will take the money to fatten my savings account, for later — a rainy day, school clothes, or vacations. Little do they know that the little bit of pocket money I keep delights me. On the way to school I treat myself to pain au chocolat, candy or some other delicacy. I am a gourmand in training, after all.

✳✳✳

The parish priest, who shall remain unnamed, has a lifestyle that I find luxurious, and this puzzles me because I have been raised with the notion that Catholic priests are humble and therefore must be poor. Not this fellow.

Indeed, Monsieur drives a nice car, lives in a lovely house that is well maintained and adjacent to the rectory, and employs the services of a gardener. Such an aristocrat. He also eats incredibly well.

One day I find myself unexpectedly in his kitchen in the late afternoon near dinner time. While we chat, he tells me that he will be preparing a simple meal that can be made swiftly; an omelet. The mere mention of this dish sets my mind and belly on fire with the thought of the porcini omelets we enjoy so much at home.

Dear Lord, please have mercy. Let me enjoy just one delicious bite of Father's meal.

But when I inquire about the possibility of special ingredients, the priest erupts.

"Absolutely not, no mushrooms," he says. "I won't be tempted by such luxuries."
There he is peeling and chopping a small shallot which he will sauté lightly in a knob of butter, but I guess these flavorful things are not luxuries. From the refrigerator, he takes four big and expensive scampis — also not a luxury —

77
_____

which he peels effortlessly and cuts into segments before tossing them into the skillet. The flesh curls slightly in the sizzling butter, and he flips them in the air majestically. Wow! Our Chef Who Art in Heaven! When the seafood is just about done, he grabs a bottle of Cognac and with a thumb on its mouth he allows a good glassful to flow into the skillet, which he has placed away from the fire. The alcohol warms instantaneously and as the skillet approaches the flame, the vapors violently ignite. I'm impressed. But not Father. He is unmoved, I gather, because he has cooked many a fine omelet and knows exactly what he is doing.

As scampis simmer over low heat, in a bowl my confessor whisks three eggs that he has flavored with salt, pepper, a bit of chives and a tablespoon of cream. While repeatedly beating the eggs, he makes conversation about an upcoming wedding. Then the conversation turns. He tells me that during certain Masses he is quite sure that attendees are a little too generous with the basket for the altar boys.

"You know, Eric, you and your brother might wish to make a charitable donation of your excess money to the church."

I'm thinking, How about I give you a few francs for half that omelet, Father Galloping Gourmet.

He goes on. "The Catholic Church, the ritual, blesses you every day. And your generosity, a small contribution, would also be a blessing to those in our parish who are less fortunate."

I tell myself, Right. Keep talking. My own father can't afford your fancy car, and last summer he commuted while his family enjoyed a vacation so that he could work to pay our bills. Oh, excuse me, Sir, do I smell butter burning?

The beaten eggs are poured into the hot iron skillet, and with a fork he scrambles the ingredients. Then he stops ministering to his non-luxuries and watches the contents gently cook.

"You know, Eric, many brilliant people with refined tastes eat their omelets as I do. Runny."

I ask myself if runny is a Latin word from the scripture, though I know it is not. This guy is getting on my nerves because I am hungry and quite sure that my prayers will not be answered. Not one delicious forkful of egg and scampi will slide down my throat. Fine! I prefer mushrooms.

78

CHAPTER TWELVE

With flawless assurance, Monsieur flips the omelet and then with his fat fist bumps the tail of the skillet, which forces the egg concoction to double over. He folds it one more time and then slides his creation onto a plate where he has placed a few leaves of seasoned green salad. For the finale, my priest tosses a knob of butter into the hot skillet; it melts instantly and then is brushed onto the omelet to give it a bright sheen. I note that by cooking on very low heat the eggs have not colored or burned. I later learn that these methods are the sign of a true connoisseur. Bravo! Can we eat now?

My priest catches me admiring his food, and I immediately feel ashamed. I'm quite sure he detects lust in my expression.

"Hungry, Eric?"

"Um. No, Father."

"Lying is a sin, is it not?"

"… Sometimes."

He arches a thick, gray eyebrow. "Sometimes?"

"I mean, yes, of course, Father, lying is a sin."

"Then let me ask one more time — "

Before he finishes his pious question he scoops a bit of omelet on a scrumptious piece of bread and flies it to my mouth, which opens wide with surprise.

Oh, God! It is succulent and, as they say in Rome, runny in a way that all brilliant people enjoy. I am struck by the combination of flavors and textures in this seafood omelet and raise my eyes to heaven in praise of the Father, the Son and the Holy Ghost.

I walk home savoring the blessing of just one taste of the buttery food. But mostly I contemplate the agile and elegant manner with which my parish priest bumped the skillet to fold the omelet. I will speak to Mamie about this technique, and then I will master it.

CHAPTER TWELVE

THIRTEEN

Foraging for Mushrooms in the Bearnese Forest

Time apparently does not heal all wounds, as the sages advise, because I am now in Grade 8 and continue to struggle in my studies. The weight of defeat is crushing my spirit as I fail English and French and muster only mediocre grades in my other subjects. The saga of my poor grades only adds to the tension at home with Dad and Mother.

"We are paying for private lessons yet your grades are still lousy. Why aren't you improving?" Dad asks.

"I am."

Mom snaps, "No, you aren't. Ask Miss Bellocks! "

"That witch hates me. It doesn't matter how hard I work. She'll never raise my grade."

This angers Dad because it sounds like a whiny excuse, and maybe it is. Yet I cannot shake the sense that I am being singled out by a mean teacher. At the same time, as I listen to my father, I realize my battle with Miss Bellock does not explain my lackluster performance in other subjects.

"You're not giving us any choice, Eric. Your mother and I agree that we'll have to find the money to send you to England in the summer. And I don't want any arguments."

I don't argue. In fact, I wish I could leave the next morning. Things are too difficult in our household. We can't be at peace or financially stable as long as Mom's health sends her back and forth between home and hospital.

Contrasting my difficulties, France is experiencing an historic electoral year which has brought a transition from right-wing to left-wing leadership with a socialist government. The dramatic presidential victory for François Mitterrand is the beginning of a fourteen-year reign that will prove controversial and more royalist than Louis XIV. His time in office will also be littered with scandals.

I will come to remember Mitterrand as a disturbing figure who in no small part defined my adolescence and early adulthood. Despite my personal doubts, we French owe many of the great architectural constructions of modern Paris to Mitterrand, particularly the Défense Arch, the Louvre Pyramid, the Opera of the Bastille, the Finance Ministry building in Bercy, and the Great Library.

And while he leads the nation, I will grow to love the television news reports about our president who always seems to eat so well, whether he is at the venerable Brasserie Lipp, the famous Maxim's, or Coupole. These Parisian establishments are all impressively decorated and inspire colorful dreams of a gastronomic world that seems impossibly inaccessible. Little do I know that one day I will actually cook for President François Mitterrand. Such a possibility seems quite remote for a teen who is stumbling through his school days. Yet I still hold onto my intention of making a career of cooking. My plan is simple: When I finish Grade 9, I will immediately enroll in culinary school so that I can train to become a chef.

✳✳✳

Despite the profound political changes taking place in France, daily life continues as usual for my family.

One Sunday morning in September Dad, Jean-Marc and I prepare to go mushroom picking in the forest with our Mamie. Jeans, anorak and rain boots are absolutely necessary. This week has provided the ideal meteorological conditions for growing mushrooms: the days have alternated between rain and sunshine. Also, our expedition falls within the period experts say is best for picking: three days before and after the new moon.

After driving in the Bearnese country side for an hour, we finally arrive at the edge of the woods near Bosdaros. It is public land with a few paths crossing into private land, but this is well marked by signs. Mushroom picking is strictly regulated in France. The mushrooms always belong to the landowner even if the land isn't fenced or identified by signs. Mushroom hunters are responsible for asking if picking is allowed in the spot they have chosen. Some municipalities limit the harvest to two or three kilograms per person, per day. In other localities, you must buy a mushroom picking permit, but we never bothered.

We pull on our boots and fill our backpacks with drinks and small pork pâté and rillettes sandwiches that Mamie prepared after a run to Mrs. Brouca, the pork butcher's wife. Dad and Mamie each carry two big flat bottom wicker baskets, as well as an Opinel folding knife. During previous outings I have learned never to put mushrooms in a plastic bag because they will ferment and, more importantly, never mix different varieties in the same basket because you risk not only crushing the most fragile mushrooms, but also contaminating your entire harvest with a toxic variety. A mushroom is identified by all its parts; that is why it must be dug out from the ground very carefully. Once we are sure it is a good, edible mushroom, we cut it at ground level with our knives.

As we head into the woods, Dad and Mamie remind us — as they often do — that we must be careful.

"Don't pick mushrooms without asking us, and especially don't put your fingers in your mouth without washing your hands first," Mamie says, and then moments later Dad repeats the very same warning.

"Yeah, yeah," Jean-Marc and I reply as we set off. We've heard it all before.

There are more lessons I learn while foraging for mushrooms with Dad and Mamie. Namely, the mushroom collector must respect nature and the environment, in this case the forests and the meadows, not to mention the landowners who allow us to harvest on their property. We are always careful not to park in their meadows, leave their fence gates open or damage their trees.

We must respect the mushrooms we pick, too, always careful not to destroy the mycelium (the vegetative part of a fungus) by digging too vigorously around

82

the mushrooms we want to pick, or by stepping on other fungi just because they are inedible or unidentifiable. And we don't just pick every edible mushroom, either. Better to leave the ones that are old or infested with parasites, rather than collecting them and throwing them away later.

The forest floor is soaked and, in some places, muddy. It is also covered with a thick layer of dead leaves, small branches, acorns, spiny chestnut seed casings and other plants. We have armed ourselves with wooden sticks to walk and to use to lift grass and ferns in order to better uncover the hidden ceps. It is early in October so not all the leaves have fallen; and despite some rays of sun piercing through the leafy trees, the forest is mostly shaded. The scent of the undergrowth, with its fragrance of wet soil, gently tickles our noses.

"It smells like ceps," says Mamie.

We all immediately sniff and inhale the air. It's true, we can smell the fungi. We spread out a little and backtrack through the woods scrutinizing each nook and cranny, moving aside leaves and ferns.

We limit our picking to only a few varieties, such as cep fungus, chanterelles and boletus. In the spring, with a bit of luck, we may also find morels on the sandy banks of the nearby Gave River, but usually only in limited quantity.

Other varieties, such as wood hedgehog, horn of plenty, and parasol mushrooms have become rare, but there is another reason we don't pick them: they have what we call "false friends," or imposters, that may be poisonous.

In France we have a way of easily avoiding the unfortunate fate of eating the wrong fungi. Pickers are welcome to take their haul into a pharmacy, because all French pharmacists are trained to identify mushroom varieties. My assumption that all pharmacists worldwide share this knowledge will be turned into a comedy sketch years later when I move to Vancouver: After fruitful foraging in a local forest, I joyfully take my pickings into a downtown drugstore only to be met with an astonished, bewildered pharmacist. The look on his face still makes me laugh, though at the time I was a bit embarrassed. Mushroom analysis, I learn, is not common practice in North American pharmacies.

Dad and Mamie take extra precautions during our foraging trips by picking only the mushrooms they know best. In these woods the ceps are considered the king of all fungi — they are highly valued because their fragrance and taste are so pleasing. They are identified by their white fleshy parts that do not turn bluish when touched; this is important, since it helps us differentiate them from the pretenders and look-alikes that can be toxic. For obvious reasons, ceps are much sought after, and we seek our fair share.

One of our favorites is the cep de Bordeaux, a majestic mushroom that can grow very big and is fairly common throughout France. In Béarn, from August to December, we find it everywhere in woods full of oak, beech and pine trees. The three other delectable varieties are rarer depending on the region.

We also like to pick chanterelles, known as girolles in France. Their fruity aroma is comparable to an apricot, and their flavor is mild. But be warned: they should never be consumed raw. The chanterelle grows in colonies from May to November in leafy and conifer woods, yet we must be careful when hunting it because the girolles attract poisonous imposters.

✳✳✳

Our eyesight quickly adjusts to the dim forest environment, and we begin to notice details that we wouldn't necessarily see if we weren't searching for mushrooms. Just walking though the forest isn't enough to find mushrooms, we must truly search for them by lifting ferns, spreading and then peering through the grass and moving the leaves and twigs. Mushrooms can grow anywhere, but they may be hiding.

While the others have already picked some ceps, I haven't found anything yet. But, eventually, my perseverance is rewarded. At the edge of a clearing, under the branches of a magnificent oak tree, I spot five ceps of Bordeaux bathed in wisps of sun. My heart is full of excitement and I yell at Dad to come and confirm my find. He checks each one of them and quickly confirms that they are quite remarkably healthy ceps that have not been attacked by worms or slugs.

"The honor is yours," he says. "Cut at ground level leaving the roots intact so the mushrooms can perhaps grow again one day."

Dad hands me the closed knife and I take hold of it carefully. When I am in the forest, or in Mamie's kitchen, or fishing from the quay in Port-Vendres, learning is a natural, joyous process. Yet when I am in the classroom, even with good teachers, learning is so difficult and I don't quite understand why. As I open the blade of the Opinel knife I wish that all my studies could occur in natural places without books and the anxiety that comes from desperately needing a good grade.

Kneeling, I cut the mushrooms one by one and place them in Dad's basket, which is already quite full. We guess that my large ceps weigh about 1.2 kilos, or nearly 3 pounds. Amazing. In less than three hours, our baskets are nearly overflowing, and we estimate that we have gathered nearly twelve kilos of fungi. Mamie is the only one who has found chanterelles. What a beautiful harvest!

We return to the car and wash our hands so that we can eat the fine sandwiches Mamie prepared for us. We don't sit in the vehicle, though, because once we get home Mom will notice every loose crumb, stem or dry leaf as though such natural things are a personal threat to her.

After our meal we spread the mushrooms out on the grass to sort them. We put the healthiest ones on one side, and on the other side we place the ones that appear to have been eaten by woodland creatures.

Back in Pau, Mom helps us clean the mushrooms indoors with a wet cloth. The healthy caps are frozen, whole and raw, in freezer bags where the freshness and taste will be kept for months.

We scrape the stems of the remaining mushrooms to remove sand and clean out any parasites or worms that may have burrowed into them. Then we slice these into big pieces along with the rest of the slightly spoiled mushrooms and caps. These we sauté in oil and butter in several uncovered frying pans over medium or, in some cases, high heat.

Once the water has evaporated, the mushrooms continue to cook in a mixture of chopped garlic and parsley, a preparation commonly called persillade. To be cautious, the mushrooms cook in the pans for at least 20 minutes. As a result, the heavenly scent of ceps will linger in the kitchen and cling to our clothing for days. If I could I would capture it in a bottle and develop my own brand of Arrouzé eau-de-toilette. What a fortune I might make!

Afterwards, we leave them to cool off in aluminum tubs where they can be kept in the freezer for up to twelve months. This will allow us to enjoy the bounty of our mushroom hunt for a whole year. I can already taste the regal omelette aux cèpes that we will undoubtedly feast on many times in the months to come.

85

CHAPTER THIRTEEN

# FOURTEEN

English Escapade:
Thank you, Miss Bellock!

I must leave my king and I wonder what Henry would think of my departure. He gave me Mamie's chicken in a pot and a marvelous garbure. And despite my lowly place in the Pau pecking order, he also provided an esteemed sense of place, tradition and lineage that makes me proud to be French. Yet it is time for me to conquer England.

The bus that will take me on a new adventure is at a standstill in the parking lot adjoining the Ursulines School, the site of my educational crucifixion. Would I prefer to be heading back to Port-Vendres in this summer of 1982? Perhaps. Yet, reluctant as I am to admit it, perhaps I have outgrown those excursions. Also, I have another motivation for crossing the English Channel. The harsh voice and words of Miss Bellocks burn my ears. "You will never be able to speak English properly!"

The parking lot is packed with cars, mostly parents bringing their children for the departure to England, where each of us will spend a couple weeks in July with a host family.

My parents walk with me to the bus while offering more advice than I can possibly retain. I am struck by the realization they are far more concerned for me than I am. Call it blissful ignorance, but I am ready for a scenic and emotional change of pace. My destination is Fareham, in the southeast of England. I carry summer clothing, notebooks and supplies for the trip, and a few packets of cake in the event my host family does not properly feed me. This is my real fear. I have heard horrid tales that the British have no cuisine, no taste, and no gastronomy. Worse, I am told that their food is always sweetened, even tomato sauce. How dare they! Maybe this is why "La Marseillaise," my national anthem, keeps playing in my head.

Allons enfants de la patrie,
  Le jour de gloire est arrivé!

We start off late in the evening and drive through the night in our modern, comfortable bus. We head toward Le Havre, about 950 km on the other side of France, where we will catch an early-morning ferry to Portsmouth.

The crossing of the English Channel — why is it not called the French Channel? — is quite exciting because of the heavy swell. Once we make it to shore, our bus continues to Fareham. The culture shock is fast and furious: These British are madmen and women who drive on the opposite side of the road!

We reach the ample parking lot of a public school and our host families are all present in expectation of our arrival. There are over one hundred people waiting and yet we are only forty-five strong. A large banner on Town Hall greets us, "Welcome to Fareham."

Our chaperons deliver each of us to a host family. The mother and father of my family are named Arden and Scott, though only Arden has come to fetch me. Her husband Scott is busy at work in the local shipyard, and the children are otherwise engaged at home. Perhaps they are too young or too old to come along with mummy. First contact with my hostess is difficult. I don't understand everything she tells me, nor does she grasp French. Our respective accents create a barrier wider than the channel I just crossed. Welcome to the United Kingdom!

Arden asks several times if she might help me carry my suitcase, which is already cutting through the flesh of my slender fingers. I politely refuse because I'm a proud Frenchman who assumes that her car is a short distance

CHAPTER FOURTEEN

away. Meanwhile, we cross many rows of vehicles without stopping, and I'm beginning to wonder if her car is parked somewhere in Scotland.

Exhaustion seizes me when we leave the confines of the parking lot and plunge into a residential neighborhood which features semi-detached homes seemingly all the way to infinity. Only now do I finally catch the meaning of what she told me as we strolled through the parking lot: "We don't own a car."

They do not own a car. What sort of family have I fallen into? My family is not among the wealthy in Pau. But Mom and Dad own a car!

Finally, after many footfalls, and long after my promise to myself that I will one day own a roller suitcase, Arden and I reach her home. Thankfully, the reception is warm, even though the children speak with an accent that does not resemble the English Miss Bellocks claims I will never learn. I understand nothing, and my new siblings, who are close to my age, watch me as though I am a rarity at the local zoo.

The first week is stressful for me. My new family does everything possible to oblige me and make me feel welcome. But the relationship is initially one-sided, because I am not capable of expressing myself in their native tongue.

Fortunately, after a week or so of complete immersion, I start to enjoy myself. One thing that I grasp quickly was the morning routine. Gary, the eldest, shows me how to purchase cigarettes for everyone in the family and where to buy beer. I am pleased to make the trek for daily supplies — three packs of cigarettes and six liters of beer. Some evenings they send me back to the store to purchase additional supplies. Truth is, they smoke like chimneys and drink with an unquenchable thirst. They do not own a car because they have all lost their drivers licenses. This, I shall not tell my parents! But I can report that everyone in this family is very kind, never actually drunk, just a little loud sometimes.

The meals are another matter. If my host mother doesn't cook properly, they don't cook at all. Breakfast is usually eggs, bacon and sausage. Midday meals are quickly cooked because they are either stir-fried or an assortment of chips — fried potatoes — savory or sweet biscuits, sandwiches and seasonal fruit. My lunch is prepared while we eat breakfast and then stuffed into a small insulated bag that I carry to school, where I attend morning English classes before eating my lunch and enjoying some cultural activities in the afternoon.

The courses are interesting and intense, quite different from the classes I experience at the Ursulines School in Pau. The instruction is animated and students are encouraged to spontaneously participate, very unlike Miss Bellocks' prison where we must request permission to breathe. These English may not have a discerning palate, but for the first time in my life I do not dread attending a language course.

It all makes me wonder why Miss Bellock, who is British, does not teach like her British brethren, who have a knack for transforming their language into something vibrant, flexible and real: The words begin to make so much sense I feel as though I might snatch them out of mid-air with my hands and stuff them down my mouth like croissant. I've never had so much fun learning, unless of course I was in Mamie's kitchen. The teachers continuously engage us with activities, such as singing and role-playing games, so that I begin to feel like a British citizen, not a flunky from France who can't speak the lingo.

The results are immediate. Very soon my understanding of this British southern accent improves, and I am somewhat able to express myself in fairly approximate English. This enables me to assist Arden, Scott and the children at dinner time.

The evening meals are truly different from those I am accustomed to at home. Mostly, they are ready-made meals purchased at McDonalds, Burger King, Pizza Hut or the corner fish and chips shop. My family is quite astonished that I know nothing of these restaurants that serve such "nutritious and delicious" food. In truth, our meals are never especially hot or particularly appetizing, though they fill my belly. Clearly, the British are a very different breed. One evening I ask where the marketplace is located. Scott says there isn't one nearby.

"Fresh produce can be purchased in Sainsbury, isn't that right, Arden?"

"Yes, Luv."

"But then you'd need a motor car to get there. Ha!"

"Eating' locally is a joy. Spurs the economy," Arden says. "Are you going to finish those chips now, Eric, or might Jason have a try?"

Jason is the youngest and about my age. We get along well and sometimes are asked to pick up our family dinners. We either share the food in the kitchen, or serve it in the living room so that everyone can gather around the television.

My new friend also introduces me to special JPS cigarettes, life at the local pub, and his mates. I seem to be a curiosity and so experience an odd sort of popularity at first. Fortunately, the lads and I are all rabid football fans, so conversation invariably diverts to the World Cup, which is underway in Spain. We spend lively evenings watching matches on TV. France is managing admirably. But much to the dismay of my hosts, England is eliminated in the second round —without having lost a game. The rules were complicated back then.

Many football fans believe the two top teams in the competition are Brazil and France. I still can recall the names of my nation's magical midfield in the summer of 1982. Platini, Giresse, Tigana and Genghini were so magical that the French team was nicknamed the "Brazilians of Europe."

The World Cup provides much to talk about at home and in the pub. The pinnacle is the final on July 11 in Madrid between Germany and Italy. A group of my classmates from France decides to gather in the local pub to watch, so I decline my host family's invitation to watch the big game with them. But when we get to the pub I'm surprised to see Gary arrive with two of his friends. We exchange greetings.

"Sorry, Eric, but the pub barkeep won't serve a bunch of French teenagers who are not accompanied by an adult. You're under age for legal consumption. But if you join us we'll see that you get your pint," he says. That was not really my plan as I never drank beer before, but suddenly, I was opened to that new experience. And what better place than a pub in England in a day of a final world cup?

His plan will work like a charm, because the pub is "family friendly", so the swamped barkeep didn't question our presence. Even so, when the first round arrives we French lads are subdued, for fear of being tossed out. Gary quickly pays the tab and we're all smiles.

As the match begins, we hoist our pints and toast to beer, country and football, although not necessarily in that order. I can't say that I love beer. Guinness and the other dark brews are too frothy and bitter. And even just a couple sips of Burton Bridge pale ale, which is more to my liking, can make me dizzy. So I drink slowly, mindful of my limits, and absorb the scene. The pub is populated mostly with fans who cheer for Germany. Unfortunately for them, Italy takes the cup.

I too feel victorious. I have conquered. I am far from the nagging confines of my Pau parents, shouting and drinking beer with adult men and women who speak a strange language I am beginning to love. Maybe I am too light-headed to think clearly; maybe I am seeing things. For a brief moment, the despicable and uniquely wicked teacher who demanded I cross a channel and personal barriers to better myself stands before me. And once again my ears burn with her toxic words: "You will never be able to speak English properly!"

As my companions cheer — goal! — I quietly sip my pale ale and whisper, "Thank you, Miss Bellocks."

$$***$$

There are only a few days left before my return to France. It has been my first true immersion in another culture. And to my great surprise I find that British culture does not revolve around food the way that it does back home. As a celebration, Arden decides to upgrade the regular meal, and purchases a steak just for me. I was so looking forward to it. I imagined a nice piece of meat sizzling into melted butter. A simple and mouth-watering vision.

"Eric, dinner is ready!"

A beautiful steak on a plate is waiting to be cooked by the stove.

As we all settle around the table, Arden seems busy and preoccupied. A large saucepan is simmering on the stove; it seems she is going to be cooking something. Maybe we are going to have some vegetables or pasta?

"Ho, Lord! Are we having steaks tonight?" Gary says.

"Ho bloody, not! Five Pounds for a steak..." his Dad answers while serving pizza to everyone. I am thinking, Pizza again!

"Five Pounds! We could have had three pizzas for that money!" Gary answers.

"French eat their meat bloody!" Scott says.

"I would never be able to swallow that," Gary answers disgusted.

Hm, I am thinking.

"Come to eat, Luv!"

Just before Arden joins us, she grabs a fork, picks up the steak and holds it for an instant before plunging it in the boiling water.

"HO!" I say, in shock and disbelief.

"What's wrong, Eric?" she asks.

I don't know what to say. I want to tell her she is nuts! One can't boil steak! They must be grilled or seared in a small amount of fat to caramelize the outside and keep the juices inside. Take it out, I want to say!

But I bite my tongue. "Nothing," I say.

Why in water, why? You cook pasta or rice in water, not a steak! How long is she going to cook it! After many long minutes, she proudly serves me the steak. It has some small pools of water over it. And it is gray, sad and it smells yucky. I know that getting a steak was a big thing for them. They wanted to please me. I can't disappoint them. They are all staring at me. So I try to smile, and force myself to keep eating. It can't be that bad, right? The meat is hard to cut and chew. It is like eating the sole of a shoe. It's disgusting, and I think that this torture will never end. But I keep on eating while smiling to my hosts, thinking about all the manners that I have learned back home. That's it, I'm ready to go back to Garbure land!

FIFTEEN

The Letter that Broke My Heart

Come August 1983 I will turn sixteen years old. Sweet sixteen? Not quite. The past three years have been very difficult at home. I harbor a secret that pains me and sears my soul.

Mom has made several suicide attempts. I don't believe they are failed attempts but rather cleverly calculated pill over-doses designed to help her escape the grim realities of our household for months at a time. Maybe she felt a compelling, irresistible need to get away from our three bedroom apartment on the fourth floor of a rather dilapidated public housing project. This life was not exactly what she had dreamed of as a little girl.

In my entire life I cannot remember a single year that has not revolved around my mother's desperate needs. Why is she so unhappy? Why does she commit acts that cause our family life to implode? Weeks of recuperation demand that we dutifully arrive at her bed after school, evenings, weekends, public holidays and school breaks.

If this question sounds harsh, it has always been balanced by my genuine sadness and concern for Mother. I want her to enjoy life more, and allow her

93

children to do the same. Unfortunately, she remains a prisoner of her despair and disappointment.

Regular hospital visits occur in the days following one of her near-death events. Then when she is moved to a clinic for several weeks of recuperation, we dutifully arrive there after school, evenings, weekends, public holidays and school breaks.

When we are not paying our respects to our fallen mother or attending class, we are at home, making do, preparing the noon meals so that we might gather and eat as a family. After our clinic visits in the evening, dinner must be prepared. Luckily, our blessing is Mamie who often welcomes us to her home for delicious food and encouragement. Then we drive home, where Jean-Marc, Christine and I plop in front of the TV, drained of emotion.

Meanwhile, Dad who has been our foundation — courageous, dedicated and hard-working — is so exhausted he can barely communicate with us. He is obviously dismayed by the endless personal drama of his princess. The ordeal has sapped him of nearly every ounce of willpower. He cannot summon the energy to help us in the ways that we have counted on, such as preparing a breakfast of biscottes with layers of butter and jam, or encouraging us to stay on top of our studies.

I have no idea if the situation at home has anything to do with my below-average school grades. From middle school through the first year of high school I have labored hard under duress and somehow, by a miracle, I have passed into the next higher class. It could be that my teachers' harsh corrections and Dad's kicks in the backside after seeing my report card have paid off. My brother and I would tremble on the day our grades arrived at home by mail. My sister Christine, who will soon be nineteen, is better at school than her brothers. Alain, our eldest sibling, must have been a good student, too, but he rarely communicates, so I can't expect any guidance from him. When I was nine he left home at age fifteen to join the air force and board at the Saintes Military School. My parents are angry with him for various reasons. I suspect Alain was simply smart enough to get out of town before he was harmed by Mother's self-destructive choices.

This has been and will continue to be a pivotal time for me. At school I have finished what is called an orientation year when students must state wishes for continuing their education. I made my intentions clear at the beginning of the school year: I am eager to earn a Certificate of Technical Education so that I might become a chef. My options for this pursuit settled on three different tourism and restaurant schools in the Pau area. The prime choice is one that is closest to our home, naturally.

If only it was a simple matter of being granted the school of my choice. Instead, the decision actually is in the hands of the school board, which assesses space availability in each school, grade point average, and the opinions of teachers. In other words, the best way to get exactly what you want is to be an excellent student.

After making my choice in the fall, I never wavered, not in January after our return from the holidays or later in March when we were expected to confirm our orientation wishes. Since my mind was made up, I went about my usual routines. Weeks and months sped by as we attended to Mother, grappled with school work and did the shopping and meal preparation to maintain some sense of normalcy at home. Then one day a crushing blow hit me harder even than Mother's suicide attempt. The teachers had warned us that letters from the school board would soon arrive, and I had butterflies in my stomach.

One day after lunch, anxious and apprehensive, I ran down the black tiled stairwell in our apartment building, taking the stair steps four at a time. At the letter box, I greet a few neighbors who are in the midst of their usual casual conversations and notice they are carrying colorful envelopes and fliers. The mail has been delivered.

On tiptoe I open the wooden letter box, but it is so high I can't see what's inside. I slip my hand in and probe. I'm excited and intrigued. Is my letter here? What will it announce? Good news or bad news? My future is likely spelled out on one single sheet of paper.

I pull out a stack of mail and without delay see colored flyers, white envelopes from the electric supply company EDF, a bound envelope for my parents from Renault — and a brown, official-looking envelope. I flip it around and startle when I see that it is addressed from the Pau School Board to my father. I want so badly to open it right then and there. But that would be wrong.

I climb the stairs as fast as I ran down. Shouting, I announce that the school letter has finally arrived. I hand it to my father. Jean-Marc and Mom watch as my father opens and reads. My stomach is tumbling as I try to interpret Dad's

95

expression.

"So? What does it say?" I ask.

He makes a sound that is gruff.

Then Mom asks, "What?"

I begin adjusting my expectations. I tell myself that I probably won't get my first choice. Okay, I can't deal with that. And maybe I won't even be granted my second best option. But I was given three possibilities and surely —

"Your orientation request for the three colleges is declined. Your academic level is to blame in the case of the first option. For the second and the third college, it's a different reason; we have to check Appendix A to see what it is."

"What does Appendix A mean?"

Dad doesn't answer. Instead, he sorts through the various sheets of information that accompany the letter. Finally, he finds what he is looking for and explains.

"This part says that since the agreements between the State education and the Private education haven't been concluded at the parliamentary spring session, all transition applications coming this year from the private system to technical public schools are delayed until September of 1983, and the start of the next academic year.

"But I was to begin my apprenticeship this summer," I say.

"That's policy, son. Truth be told, the political left has been in power for a year now for the first time since 1958 and things are in a shambles."

I recall the mass euphoria on May 10 1981 when election results were announced.

Dad goes on. "But, well, they say here that you are pre-approved for the following vocational training."

After he has finished reading, I take the letter in my own hands because I cannot fathom what I have just heard. The letter lists these opportunities:

- Hairdresser at the technical school of Mourenx (30 km from home)
- Accountant
- Plumber
- Bulldozer driver for the construction of new Highway A64
- Masonry and construction worker

The letter instructs us to notch a box that designates our choice within seven days, the official postmark deadline. There is no possibility to appeal.

Everything around me becomes a blur. I notice that my father is as shocked as I am, and this pains me because I know how hard he has worked to send his children to good schools. I argue with the letter as if the school board is in the room with us. I express outrage at not being able to fulfill what I have chosen to do with my life.

For years I have been a gourmand in training. And now technocrats are telling me no. You must become a plumber, a hairdresser or drive a bulldozer. I am in hell. I feel as though I have died. Distraught, I take refuge in my room and curl up on my bed. The tears and pain won't stop. Mamie comes to mind and I can't bear the thought of her disappointment.

Then I hear my mother. I look up and see her frail body looming over me.

"You get what you deserve. That'll teach you. You just have to work better at your school grades."

Her words hurt, add to my humiliation, but I don't dare speak. We have been taught not to argue with Mother; even Dad, a strong man, finds it easier to be passive rather than confront her.

My dream of becoming a chef disappears with the last rays of daylight. My mood is dark; I wish I could tear down the school board building. Not even sixteen years of age and yet my future has been extinguished by a bunch of strangers, people I have never met and who don't really know me.

I curse our poverty and believe that if I had been born into a wealthy family we would not be suffering in this way. And the vocational choices I've been given are, in my mind, a road to more poverty and disillusionment.

97

Finally, exhausted, I am ready to surrender to sleep when a calm voice deep within me whispers, You will find a way.

Of course, I did find a way. But not until after a disastrous visit to the school administration building where I was ejected by guards. Crying on a park bench, beyond despair, I had a moment of clarity — a revelation — that would carry me through the next stage of my professional development. I would call the best restaurants in Pau, ask to speak to the chef and then announce, "It would be my honor to become your apprentice."

I must leave the details of my continuing saga for another day, and the next Child to Chef book. But, by sixteen, the foundations of my culinary training were solidly laid and my basic repertoire of dishes established. Never give up. Never!

RECIPES

lb	pound
oz	ounce
fl oz	fluid ounce
ml	mililitre
l	litre
g	gram
kg	kilogram
tbsp	tablespoon
tsp	teaspoon
°F	degrees Fahrenheit
°C	degrees Celsius

Visit www.childtochef.com for the book pictures, recipes and updates.

Classic Sangria

Sangria is a light alcoholic beverage made with red wine, fruit juice, sparkling soft drinks, sugar, and fruit chunks. Sometimes liqueurs are added, as well as cinnamon. It is hard to find two sangrias that taste the same as there is no single specific recipe for it.

Estimated time to complete: 2 hours, 5 minutes   Serves: 4

2 tbsp (30 ml) Brandy
1 lemon, sliced and quartered thinly
1 orange, sliced and quartered thinly
1/2 lime, sliced and quartered thinly
1.5 cups (350 ml) red wine
1/2 cup (120 ml) port wine
1/2 tsp (2.5 ml) cinnamon powder
1/ 16 tsp (pinch) clove powder
2 tbsp (30 ml) pure vanilla extract
1/3 cup (70 g) sugar
1.5 cups (350 ml) soda water
6 to 8 ice cubes

In a bowl, use a wooden spoon to mix the citrus slices with the Brandy and sugar. Add the red wine, port wine, cinnamon, cloves, and vanilla. Stir until sugar is dissolved. Transfer to a punch bowl, chill until ready to serve, then stir in soda water and add ice cubes.

Mamie Augusta's Garbure

Whenever I share memories of Mamie's cooking lessons, my mouth begins to water. If you enjoyed reading about my grandmother, I'm sure you'll want to try her delicious garbure.

Garbure is a traditional dish from the Pyrénées, more specifically from Bigorre. It was the dish of the poor and most often served as their only main daily meal. It is a type of vegetable hotpot made, for the most part, of white beans added to the bone of a ham for flavor. Traditionally, it was served as a soup on rancid bread slices because in Bigorre, bread isn't discarded.

Far from its humble origins, today the garbure has become one of the most fashionable regional dishes. It is good practice, about 30 minutes before serving, to add pieces of goose, duck, or pork confit. Some Bearnese and Basques imitate the people of nearby region La Corréze by making chabrot which consists of eating nearly all the soup on the plate, adding a glass of red wine to the rest, and drinking it right from the plate.

Estimated time to complete: 3 hours, 30 minutes   Serves: 8 to 10

1/2 lb (225 g) Bayonne ham, diced
1/2 lb (225 g) smoked bacon, diced
2/3 lb (225 g) dried white beans (Tarbais beans if possible)
Note: Beans must be left to soak in water overnight.
1/4 cup (60 ml) duck fat
1 lb (450 g) diced onions, (approx. 2 onions)
2/3 lb (225 g) leeks, thinly sliced (approx. 2 leeks)
1 small green cabbage, thinly sliced
1-1/2 lbs (680 g) potatoes cut in large cubes
1 lb (450 g) sliced carrots (approx. 3 or 4 carrots)
1 lb (450 g) diced turnips (approx. 2 turnips)
1 bouquet garni
6 cloves garlic, chopped
1 tsp (5 ml) marjoram, chopped
1 tsp (5 ml) Espelette pepper
2.2 lbs duck conserve (1 kg) - about 2 legs and wings confit in duck fat
Salt and ground pepper
Optional (in season) 1/2 lb (225 g) green beans cut in one-inch pieces
Soak the Tarbais beans in cold water overnight. Rinse and drain them thoroughly.

Place the ham heel and smoked pork into 3 liters (about 3 quarts) of water. Cook and simmer for about 30 minutes. Add the drained Tarbais beans and simmer for an hour. Skim occasionally.

Warm up the duck fat in a large stewpot over medium heat. Add the diced onions, leeks, and cabbage. Stir for 10 minutes to brown them, but be careful not to cook them through. Add the , potatoes, carrots, turnips, bouquet garni, garlic, marjoram, Espelette pepper, duck conserve, salt and ground pepper. Incorporate the beans and smoked ham. Mix thoroughly and bring to a boil. The vegetables must be generously covered with water up to 5 centimeters (about 2 inches) above the vegetables. Add a little water as needed. Simmer for about two hours, stirring occasionally. Fifteen minutes before serving, add the string beans (if using).

Before serving, remove the bouquet garni. Remove the conserve and separate the meat from the bones. Add the shredded meat to the soup. Mix and serve the hot soup in a tureen.

Note: Once you master the secrets of making a delicious garbure, you may participate in the official garbure world contest, La Garburade, which takes place every year in Béarn at Oloron-Sainte-Marie at mid-September every year.

Marinated Olives

A Spanish cook is just as likely to buy marinated olives as to prepare his or her own as the variety of prepared olives is so vast, there are endless flavour combinations from which to choose.

Estimated time to complete: 5 days   Serves: 6

1/2 cup (120 ml) green olives in brine, cracked and well rinsed
1/2 cup (120 ml) black olives in brine, cracked and well rinsed
1 broiled, peeled and seeded red bell pepper, thinly sliced
1 lemon, halved and thinly sliced
1/4 tsp (1.25 ml) dry oregano
1/4 tsp (1.25 ml) dry thyme leaves
1/4 tsp (1.25 ml) dry basil
1/4 tsp (1.25 ml) dry fennel seeds, ground
1/2 tsp (2.5 ml) coriander seeds, cracked lightly
1/2 tsp (2.5 ml) whole peppercorns, cracked lightly
2 bay leaves
1 red hot chilli
About 1/2 (120 ml) cup extra virgin olive oil

Place all ingredients in a bowl except the olive oil, and mix well. Transfer the olives and marinade to a 1-cup preserving jar and pour enough oil over to cover. Seal the jar and set aside at room temperature, protected from natural light for 5 to 7 days, before using. Turn the jar over every day; the movement liberates the flavors of the spices.

Food Safety Tip: Do not add sliced garlic to an oil marinade such as this because of the possibility of botulism infection. If you want a garlic flavour, use a commercially prepared garlic-flavoured olive oil instead.

If you store the marinade in the fridge, the oil will congeal and turn opaque in color. It will clear again as it returns to room temperature.

Paprika Spiced Almonds

In Spain, almonds are prepared in many ways and are a popular snack with drinks. They are often included in a selection of tapas and served with Sherry, wine, or other drinks. This version adds the piquant flavour of paprika. These almonds will keep up to 3 days in an airtight container.

Estimated time to complete: 16 minutes   Makes: 1/2 lb

3/4 tsp (3.6 ml) coarse sea salt
1/4 tsp (1.2 ml) smoked sweet paprika powder*
2 whole black peppercorns
1 cup (250 ml) blanched almonds
1 tsp (5 ml) extra virgin olive oil

Preheat oven to 400°F / 200°C with rack in middle.

Put the sea salt, paprika, and peppercorns in a mortar and grind with the pestle to a fine powder.

Place the almonds on a baking sheet and toast in a preheated oven for about 6 to 8 minutes, stirring occasionally until golden brown and giving off a toasted aroma; watch carefully after 5 minutes as almonds burn quickly. When done, immediately transfer to a heatproof bowl.

Drizzle about half a teaspoon of olive oil over top and stir to ensure all the nuts are lightly and evenly coated; add extra oil if necessary. Sprinkle with the sea salt and paprika mixture and stir well again. Spread out and let cool before transferring to a small bowl to serve at room temperature.

* Smoked Spanish paprika is a powerful flavor and is essential in Spanish cuisine. Whole peppers are dried slowly over an oak burning fire for several weeks. The result is a sweet, cool, smoky flavor that is available mild or hot.

Spanish Tortilla

For this recipe, low-starch potatoes work best. I've used everything from small red potatoes to oblong Idaho russets in tortillas. Any potato will do the job but I prefer boiling potatoes, red potatoes, or Yukon Gold best because they have lower starch content and don't fall apart during frying. I also prefer their firmer texture. If you have a mandolin, this is a great time to use it.

Estimated time to complete: 30 minutes   Serves: 4 as tapas

1/4 cup (60 ml) vegetable oil for frying
1 medium Yukon Gold potato
1/4 tsp coarse salt
1/2 medium onion, diced
2 garlic cloves, chopped
2 large eggs
1/16 tsp freshly ground black pepper

In a large, non-stick skillet that is at least 1-1/2 inches deep, heat the oil on medium high. While oil is heating, slice the potatoes thinly, about 1/8 inch. Transfer to a bowl and sprinkle on 1/4 teaspoons of the salt, tossing to distribute it well.

When the oil is very hot gently slip the potatoes into the oil with a skimmer or slotted spoon. Fry the potatoes, turning occasionally (trying not to break them) and adjusting the heat so they sizzle but don't crisp or brown. Set a sieve or colander over a bowl and, when the potatoes are tender, after about 8 to 10 minutes, transfer them into the sieve.

Add the onions and garlic to the pan. Fry on low heat, stirring occasionally, until the onions are very soft and translucent but not browned; about 4 to 6 minutes. Remove pan from the heat and using the skimmer, transfer onions and garlic to the sieve with the potatoes. Drain the oil from the skillet, setting aside at least a tablespoon, and wipe out the pan with a paper towel so it's clean. Scrape out any stuck-on bits if necessary.

In a large bowl, beat the eggs, salt, and pepper with a fork until blended. Add the drained potatoes, onions, and garlic and mix gently to combine with the egg, being careful not to break the potatoes.

Heat the skillet on medium high. Add the tablespoon of reserved oil. It is important to let the pan and oil get very hot first so that the eggs don't stick. Once pan is hot, pour in the potato and egg mixture, spreading it evenly. Cook for 1 minute and then lower heat to medium low, cooking until the eggs are completely set at the edges and halfway set in the centre, and the tortilla easily slips around in the pan when you give it a shake, about 6 to 8 minutes. You may need to nudge the tortilla loose with a knife or spatula.

Set a flat, rimless plate that's at least as wide as the skillet upside down over the pan. Lift the skillet off the burner and with one hand against the plate and the other holding the skillet's handle, invert the skillet so the tortilla lands on the plate. Set the pan back on the heat and slide the tortilla into it, using the skimmer to push any stray potatoes back in under the eggs as the tortilla slides off the plate. Once the tortilla is back in the pan, tuck the edges in and under to neaten the sides. Cook until a skewer inserted into the centre comes out clean, hot, and with no uncooked egg on it, another 5 to 6 minutes.

Transfer the tortilla to a serving platter and let cool at least 5 minutes. Serve warm, at room temperature, or slightly cool. Cut into wedges or small squares, sticking a toothpick in each square if serving as an appetizer.

Mussels with Herbs
and Garlic Butter

Due to the lack of lush pastureland in most of Spain, dairy cattle are not commonly raised and therefore, oil, as opposed to butter, is more commonly used in cooking. Nevertheless, butter is occasionally used, as in this recipe, but can be substituted with olive oil if you so choose.

Estimated time to complete: 25 minutes   Serves: 6

1 lb (450 g) large fresh mussels in their shells
1/4 cup (60 ml) dry white wine
1 bay leaf
2 oz (60 g) butter
1/4 cup (60 ml) coarsely chopped breadcrumbs
2 tbsp (30 ml) chopped flat parsley, plus extra sprigs to garnish
1 1/2 tbsp (10 g) chopped fresh chives
2 garlic cloves, finely chopped
Salt and pepper
Lemon wedges to serve

Preheat oven to 425°F / 220°C with rack in middle.

Clean mussels by scraping their shells and pulling out the beards. Discard any mussels with broken shells. Put mussels in a strainer and rinse under cold running water.

Place mussels in a large pan; add a splash of wine and the bay leaf. Cook covered, over high heat for 5 minutes, shaking the pan occasionally, or until the mussels are opened. Drain and discard any mussels that remain completely closed.

Shell the mussels, setting aside one half of each shell. Arrange mussels in their half shells in a large, shallow, ovenproof serving dish.

Melt the butter and pour into a small bowl. Add the breadcrumbs, parsley, chives, garlic, and salt and pepper to taste; mix together well.

Let stand until the butter has set slightly. Using your fingers or a spoon, take a large pinch of the herb butter mixture and use it to fill each mussel shell, pressing down well. You can chill the filled mussels in the refrigerator at this point until ready to serve.

To serve, bake the mussels in the oven for 10 minutes or until very hot. Serve immediately, garnished with parsley sprigs and lemon wedges for squeezing atop.

The Priest's Omelette

A decadent mushroom omelette recipe with hints of Cognac and cream perfectly rolled and not overcooked, like a French chef or priest might master. Alternatively, you may substitute the chives with basil or tarragon and the scampi with lobster or shrimp.

Estimated time to complete: 15 minutes   Serves: 1

2 tsp (10 ml) grape seed oil
3 free range eggs
1/2 tbsp (5 g) chopped chives
2 tbsp (30 ml) crème fraîche or heavy cream
1 tbsp (15 g) chopped shallot
2 to 3 large scampi or jumbo prawns
2 tbsp (30 ml) of Cognac or Brandy
Salt and freshly ground pepper to taste
1/2 tsp (2.5 ml) butter

Briefly blanch the scampi in boiling salted water for about 30 seconds and refresh in ice cold water. Remove the shells and cut the tails into half inch pieces.

In a bowl, beat the eggs, seasoning, and chives with a fork for about a minute or until slightly foamy.

Heat the oil in the omelette pan, add the chopped shallot and cook for about a minute without browning. Add the diced scampi and cook on low heat for a minute then flame with Cognac. Add the crème fraîche and simmer for a few minutes or until sauce has thickened.

Briefly beat the eggs again and add to the pan. Turn the heat down to low and use a fork to scramble the stir the eggs. As the eggs set on the outer edges of the pan, use a fork (or a wooden spatula if you are using a non stick pan) and draw them toward the center of the pan. Repeat as needed while shaking the pan to allow any uncooked liquid set and cook until eggs almost form a large pancake. With a spatula, lift up and fold. When the omelette sets, slide onto a serving dish. Fold a second time to create a rolled shape with the omelette.

Wipe the pan with a piece of paper towel then add butter to melt. Brush the top of the omelette with the melted butter to make it shiny; this is called to "lustrate" the omelet - it's a must in the art of omelet making.

Serve immediately.

Ceps Persillade

Persil is the French word for "parsley" and persillade is a mixture of chopped parsley and garlic. It is usually added as a flavoring or garnish to dishes just before cooking is complete. What a delicious way to eat your mushrooms!

Estimated time to complete: 25 minutes   Serves: 4

1 lb (450 g) ceps or mixed mushrooms
1 tbsp (15 ml) vegetable oil
1 tbsp (15 ml) butter
1 shallot, chopped
2-3 cloves garlic, chopped
2 tbsp (15 g) chopped parsley
Salt and pepper, to taste

Pick through mushrooms to discard leaves and twigs. Trim mushroom stems and brush them to remove grit. If very dirty, wash them by tossing in a large bowl of cold water, and then lift them out with your hands so grit falls to bottom. Do not leave them to soak or they will absorb water. Cut any large mushrooms in 2-3 pieces and drain them in a colander.

Peel and finely chop the shallot and garlic and put to one side of the chopping board. Chop the parsley, add shallot and garlic, and chop them briefly together. Stir in a bowl and reserve; this is what we call the persillade.

Sauté mushrooms in a large pan with oil and butter until mushrooms are soft and brown. Add persillade and sauté for 5 to 7 minutes. Serve as a garnish for soup or in omelettes.

Ceps Omelette

A beautiful mushroom omelette recipe with hints of garlic and parsley, perfectly rolled and not overcooked. Don't forget to lustrate, as was done with the priest omelet!

Estimated time to complete: 25 minutes   Serves: 4

3 free range eggs
2 tbsp (30 ml) cream
Salt and freshly ground pepper, to taste
1/2 tbsp (8 ml) butter
1/2 cup (120 ml) cooked ceps in persillade

Combine the eggs, cream, pepper, and salt, and beat lightly. In your favorite omelette pan, melt the butter. Pour the egg mixture into the pan. Scatter your mushroom fillings atop the eggs, in the center. As the eggs set on the outer edges of the pan, use a fork (or a wooden spatula if you are using a non stick pan) and draw them toward the center of the pan. Repeat as needed while shaking the pan to allow any uncooked liquid set and cook until eggs almost form a large pancake. With a spatula, lift up and fold. When the omelette sets, slide onto a serving dish. Fold a second time to create a rolled shape with the omelette.

Wipe the pan with a piece of paper towel then add an extra teaspoon of butter to melt in the pan. Brush the top of the omelette with the melted butter to add shine and flavor.

Serve immediately.

Chicken Croquettes With Romesco Sauce

Of all croquettes, chicken croquettes are the most popular. In northern Spain, croquettes are usually made with cod, in Andalucía it is ham, and in the Balearic Islands and Catalonia they use monkfish (anglerfish). You can adapt this basic recipe in many ways, using a range of other meats . Sauce recipe is included on the next page.

Estimated time to complete: 40 minutes   Serves: 6

5 oz (140 g) chicken breast, skinned and boned
Olive oil
1/2 tbsp (7.5 ml) butter
3/4 tbsp (11 ml) all-purpose flour
1/2 cup (120 ml) milk
Salt and freshly ground pepper, to taste
A pinch of grated nutmeg
1 tbsp (5 g) of chopped oregano
1 tbsp (5 g) of chopped parsley
3 small eggs, separated
Cornmeal

Wash the chicken, pat dry with kitchen paper, and fry in a little olive oil for 8 to 10 minutes over low heat. When cooked, remove and set aside.

Melt the butter in a saucepan and add the flour. Stir with a wire whisk until mixture thickens. Gradually add the milk to the roux mixture, whisking constantly until you have a smooth, thick sauce. Season with salt, pepper, and nutmeg. Remove from heat and set aside.

Mince the chicken in a blender, and fold with 3 egg yolks into the white sauce. Reserve the whites. Add the chopped parsley and oregano.

Mix the reserved whites with the remaining eggs. Using a spoon, put 6 equal sized portions of the croquette mixture on a cookie sheet. Chill for about 10 minutes. Coat with flour, dip into the beaten eggs, and roll in cornmeal. Fry the croquettes in batches in hot olive oil until golden brown. Reserve in a warm oven and serve hot.

112

Romesco Sauce

This Catalan tomato sauce is traditionally served with fish and shellfish but it is also ideal to serve as a dipping sauce. Authentic recipes are made with dried Romesco chillies, which have a sweet, hot flavour. Unfortunately they are difficult to obtain outside the region.

Estimated time to complete: 2 hours, 35 minutes   Makes: 3/4 cup

2 large ripe tomatoes, cored and cut in half
10 blanched almonds
2 large garlic cloves, unpeeled and whole
1 small dried sweet chilli, soaked for 20 minutes
Pinch of sugar
1/3 cup (80 ml) extra virgin olive oil
1 tbsp red wine vinegar
Salt and pepper

Preheat oven to 375°F / 190°C with rack in middle.

Place the tomatoes and garlic on a baking sheet and roast in preheated oven for 20 minutes. Add the almonds during the last 5 minutes until they are golden and giving off an aroma - be sure to keep an eye on them so they don't burn!

Peel the roasted garlic and tomatoes. Put the almonds, garlic, and sweet chillies in a food processor and process until finely chopped. Add the tomatoes and sugar and process again.

With the motor running, slowly add the olive oil through the feed tube. Add the vinegar and quickly process. Taste and rectify the seasoning if desired.

Let stand for at least 2 hours then serve at room temperature. Alternatively, cover and let chill for up to 3 days and then bring to room temperature before serving. Stir before serving to blend any oil that may have separated.

Duck Rillettes au Torchon

Mr. Brouca, the pork butcher, would approve of this simple duck rillette recipe, despite my use of meat from duck legs, as this recipe is usually made using mainly the meat from the wings and neck. As a young cook I altered the original recipe because I would not learn to make duck confit until years later.

Estimated time to complete: 2 hours   Serves: 12

10 duck legs confit, well cooked
6 shallots, finely chopped
2/3 lb (300 g) black trumpet mushrooms*, sliced if large
3 tbsp (45 ml) duck fat
1 tbsp (15 ml) butter
1 tbsp (15 ml) finely chopped chives
1 tbsp (15 ml) finely chopped parsley
1 black truffle, finely chopped
2 tbsp (30 ml) black truffle oil
1 tsp (5 ml) Quatre-Épices powder
Salt and white pepper, to taste

Warm the duck legs and shred with your hands. Sauté shallots and mushrooms in duck fat and butter until tender. Add to duck meat and mix in the herbs, minced truffle, and truffle oil. Season with salt, white pepper, and Quatre-Épices powder to taste.

Form the duck rillettes into roulades and roll in plastic wrap. Make cylindrical rolls about 6 inches long and 2 to 2-1/2 inches wide. Refrigerate for at least 1 hour and then slice and serve with a crusty bread.

Note: Quatre-Épices powder is a mixture of nutmeg, cloves, ginger, and white pepper, and is available at specialty food stores.

*You may substitute with other preferred wild mushrooms, such as boletus and morel.

Dad's Mustard Rabbit Dish

This is another of Dad's favourite recipes that I have tweaked over the years by adding artichokes and olives.

Estimated time to complete: 2 hours   Serves: 6

1 rabbit cut into 12 pieces - You can ask your butcher to do this for you.
Salt and black pepper
1/4 cup (30 g) all-purpose flour
3 tbsp (45 ml) butter
1/4 cup (60 ml) brandy
1/2 lb (225 g) small whole mushrooms, washed
1/2 lb (225 g) cooked marinated artichoke hearts, rinsed
1/4 cup (50 g) olives, pitted
Juice of 1 lemon, freshly squeezed
2 cups (1/2 l) chicken stock
4 thinly sliced green onions
1/4 cup (25 g) chopped fresh tarragon leaves
1 cup (1/4 l) whipping cream
3 tbsp (45 ml) Dijon mustard
3 tbsp (45 ml) mustard seeds
1/4 cup (25 g) minced parsley
Preheat oven to 375°F / 190°C.

Season the rabbit pieces with salt and pepper; coat with flour. Melt the butter in a wide frying pan over medium-high heat. Cook the rabbit a few pieces at a time until brown on all sides. Drain the fat and discard it.

Move frying pan into an open area, away from exhaust fans and flammable items. Add brandy and ignite; shake pan until flame dies. Transfer rabbit to a shallow 4-quart baking pan. Melt a fresh knob of butter in the frying pan over medium heat. Add mushrooms and cook slightly, stirring often and deglazing with chicken stock. Pour over the rabbit. Add the chopped tarragon and sliced green onions. Cover and bake in preheated oven about 45 to 55 minutes or until rabbit is tender.

In the frying pan, stir in lemon juice, cream, mustard seeds, Dijon mustard, and the remaining juices from the baking pan and bring to a boil. Add the marinated artichokes and pitted olives and cook for about 10 minutes or until the sauce has thickened. Taste and rectify the seasoning with salt and pepper as needed. Transfer rabbit to a serving dish. Pour sauce over rabbit, sprinkle with chopped parsley, and serve immediately.

115

King Henry's Poule au pot

When you prepare this dish, please remember my dear Mamie and her love of French history. You might also want to salute the kind king who would smile to know you are about to eat so well!

To begin, order a two year old chicken. Ask for a bird with a minimal body cavity opening in order to sew it easily.

Estimated time to complete: 3 hours, 45 minutes   Serves: 8

5.5 – 6.6 lbs (2.5 to 3 kg) hen
1 lb (450 g) carrots, peeled
1 onion peeled with 4 cloves inserted
3 medium turnips, peeled
1 cabbage with leaves separated, washed, and re-tied with kitchen string
1 Bouquet Garni*
Gizzard and neck of the chicken
2/3 lb (300 g) white bread, cut into cubes
1 cup (240 ml) milk
2 tbsp (30 ml) Cognac
1 chicken liver, ground
1/2 lb (225 g) veal scallop, ground
1/4 lb (115 g) cured ham, ground
1/2 lb (225 g) smoked bacon, ground
4 cloves garlic, ground
2 shallots, ground
15 parsley sprigs, leaves stripped from stems, chopped
1 tsp (5 ml) thyme leaves, chopped
3 leeks, washed and tied together
2 eggs
Salt and ground black pepper, to taste

Empty the chicken cavity, reserving the gizzard and neck, and return chicken to the fridge.

To prepare the broth, place the carrots, onion, turnips, cabbage, bouquet garni, gizzard, and neck in a large stew pot. Cover with cold water by at least an inch. Bring water to a boil then lower heat and simmer for 45 minutes.

116

While the stock is simmering, prepare the stuffing. In a big bowl, mix the white bread, milk, and Cognac. Let mixture sit 5 minutes, then knead the mixture well by hand.

Use a mincer to –grind the liver, veal, ham, bacon, garlic, shallots, parsley, thyme. Add the minced mixture to the bread mixture. Break the eggs in a bowl, season with salt and ground pepper, and mix well. Fill the chicken cavity with the stuffing, and, using a trussing needle, sew up the opening to keep the stuffing inside.

Add the stuffed chicken and the tied leeks to the broth, completely covering the chicken. Add more water if necessary. Cover with a lid, bring to a boil on high heat, then lower heat to maintain a simmer. Cook slowly for about two hours, perhaps even longer. The tip of a knife must penetrate the flesh effortlessly.

Remove chicken from the stock pot and carve it, along with the stuffing. Serve chicken with the sliced stuffing surrounded by vegetables and Italian style tomato sauce in a sauceboat.

*The Bouquet Garni (French for "garnished bouquet") is a bundle of herbs usually tied together with a string to prevent them from dispersing in the liquid. The bundle is mainly used to prepare soup, stock, and various stews, and can be tied to the green part of a leek or housed in a piece of cheesecloth. The bouquet is boiled with the other ingredients but is removed prior to consumption. Occasionally, when the liquid is going to be strained, a loose bouquet can be added.

While there is no generic recipe for Bouquet Garni, most include parsley, thyme, bay leaf, the green part of a leek, and whole black peppercorns. Depending on the meal you are preparing, the Bouquet Garni may include basil, thyme, chervil, rosemary, peppercorns, savory, and/or tarragon.

Paella of Barcelona

Paella is a Spanish dish of saffron-flavoured rice combined with a variety of meats, including chorizo, and shellfish such as shrimp, scallops, squid, crabmeat, mussels, and clams as well as garlic, onions, peas, artichoke hearts and tomatoes. It is named after the special two-handled pan, called the paella, in which it is prepared and served. The pan is wide, shallow and 13 to 14 inches in diameter.

Estimated time to complete: 1 hour, 20 minutes   Serves: 8

2 mild pork sausages, sliced
1 chicken breast, cut into 1/2 inch diced
1/2 lb (225 g) firm fish cut into 1 inch pieces
1/2 lb (225 g) medium sized shrimp, peeled
1/4 lb (110 g) scallops
1/2 lb (225 g) squid, cleaned and cut into 1 inch rings
1/4 lb (110 g) crabmeat, roughly 1-2 inch chunks
12 mussels, clean
12 clams, clean
1/4 lb (110 g) chorizo cut in 1/4 inch slices
3 tbsp (45 ml) olive oil
1 medium onion, chopped
1 red bell pepper, cut into 1 inch slices
4 cloves garlic, minced
1 tsp (15 ml) paprika
2 g saffron
Salt & pepper, to taste
1 large tomato, finely chopped
3 cups (3/4 l) short-grain rice
1 can artichoke hearts, drained
5 oz. (140 g) frozen peas, thawed

Preheat oven to 375° F/ 190°C with rack just below the middle.

Select a large oven proof skillet to be used for the sautéing, baking, and serving. In 1 inch of water, steam clams and mussels until just opened. Remove them immediately. Combine the water from the steaming, the clam juice, and enough extra water to make 5 and 1/2 cups of liquid and bring to a boil.

Sauté the sausages and chicken until cooked, if not already cooked. Remove the sausages and chicken and set aside. Sauté the onions, red pepper, and garlic in olive oil until soft. Stir in the paprika, saffron, salt, and pepper. Add the tomato to the peppers and sauté until hot. Stir in the uncooked rice and sauté 3-5 minutes. Add the hot clam juice and mix well. Cook over moderate heat, uncovered, for 5 minutes without stirring.

Stir in the chorizo, squid, crabmeat, and fish. Pat the entire top into a flat, even, but still loose surface. Arrange the shrimp, scallops, and artichokes and press into the rice. Bake uncovered for 15 min, or until rice and seafood are just cooked. Arrange and press the clams and mussels, open side up, into the rice. Sprinkle peas over top. Bake for 5 more min and serve immediately.

Note: All of the above meats/seafoods and quantities are just a suggestion; use whatever is to your liking and is available - the more variety, the more fun! However, do not use oysters as their unique taste clashes with the others.

Paella pan facts: The most important characteristic of this pan is its large surface, which facilitates the rapid evaporation of cooking liquid, allowing that wonderfully brown and crunchy final rice product (referred to by Spaniards as "soccarat") to develop. Paella pans come in different sizes and are made of diverse materials from iron to stainless steel; you should choose one based on your individual preference and the amount of people you plan to regularly serve. As a general rule, a 16 inch pan serves 4-5 guests. To avoid the annoyance of rusting, when you first purchase your pan, and after every subsequent usage, it's a good idea to boil a simple mix of water and vinegar, then dry it and rub with olive oil.

Dad's Recipe for Bœuf Braisé aux Carottes

I remember waking one Sunday morning to the aroma of onions, sautéed meat, wine, and spices simmering in the kitchen. As I approached, the smell was so strong that my mouth began to water. I was surprised to find Dad cooking this splendid dish. He was already cleaning up the kitchen after assembling the food and placing it in a cast-iron casserole.

Estimated time to complete: 3 hours   Serves: 8

2 tbsp (30 ml) vegetable oil (Dad used peanut oil, I prefer grape seed oil)
1 tbsp (15 ml) butter
3 lbs (1.2 kg) boneless stew beef, such as chuck, top or bottom round, cut into 1 1/2-inch pieces
Salt and pepper, to taste
1/4 cup (30 g) all-purpose flour
2 onions, halved and thinly sliced
5 cloves of garlic, chopped
2 tbsp (30 ml) tomato paste
1 lb (450 g) carrots, cut into 1-inch pieces
2 cups (1/2 l) dry white wine
3 cups (3/4 l) cold water, or more if necessary
3 sprigs fresh thyme
2 bay leaves
1/4 cup (25 g) mixed fresh herbs (parsley, basil, chives)

Mix flour with half a teaspoon each of salt and pepper. Add a tablespoon each of the oil and butter to a large cast iron casserole over medium heat. Dredge half of the meat in the flour mix to coat. Tap the meat to remove excess flour then add it to the hot fat in the casserole. Sear the meat, without moving it, for 3 to 4 minutes or until brown. Flip and brown the other side for 3 to 4 minutes. Remove meat from the pan and brown the remaining meat in the same way; remove it from the pan with cooking juices.

Add the remaining tablespoon of oil to the pan. Add the onions and garlic and cook, stirring often, for 5 minutes. Add the carrots and cook 2 minutes more. Add the white wine and tomato paste then return the meat and its juices to the pan.
Add the water - it should just cover the meat - with the thyme, bay leaves, salt, and pepper. Bring to a boil then lower the heat and cover the pan.

Simmer, stirring occasionally, for 2 hours or until the meat is very tender when pierced with the point of a knife. Serve with noodles tossed in butter. Garnish with chopped fresh herbs.

120

Grilled Sardines with Lemon Sauce

Dad was very good at grilling the sardines but to be honest, he never made this sauce - it's my personal touch!

Estimated time to complete: 25 minutes   Serves: 4

1/4 cup (60 ml) melted butter or extra virgin olive oil
Juice of a lemon, strained
1 small shallot, finely chopped
2 garlic cloves, finely chopped
1 tbsp (15 ml) chopped chives
2 tbsp (30 ml) fresh parsley, finely chopped
Sea salt and ground black pepper to taste
24 fresh sardines, cleaned and gutted
Sea salt and ground black pepper to taste
2 tbsp (30 ml) extra virgin olive oil
1 lemon, cut into 8 wedges

Preheat a medium hot grill or BBQ.

In a small pot, combine melted butter, lemon juice, chopped shallot, and garlic. Simmer gently for a couple of minutes. Remove from heat and add the chopped parsley, chives, and seasoning.

Wipe the grill with some vegetable oil to clean it. Season sardines with a little olive oil and a sprinkle of salt and pepper. When grill is hot, place sardines between two racks, ensuring you can flip them easily. Grill until fish are cooked through and nicely charred, about 2-3 minutes per side.

Remove fish from grill and place on a platter. Drizzle butter sauce over the sardines. Serve the remaining sauce on the side along with extra lemons wedges. Serve warm - don't forget to appreciate the beautiful aromas of the dish!

Conger Eel Provencal

If you can not find conger eel, you may substitute with ling cod steaks. Easy and succulent, this sauce is perfect for fish, shellfish, poultry and pasta.

Estimated time to complete: 1 hour, 15 minutes   Serves: 6

6 conger eel slices, 1.5 inches thick
2 tbsp (30 ml) flour
1/4 tsp (pinch) fine sea salt
1/4 tsp (pinch) ground black pepper
1 tbsp (15 ml) Herbes de Provence
3 tbsp (45 ml) extra virgin olive oil
1 onion, chopped
2 garlic cloves, thinly chopped
1 cup (240 ml) dry white wine
4 cups (1 l) tomatoes, peeled, seeded, and chopped
1/8 tsp (pinch) cayenne pepper powder
1 bay leaf
1/2 tsp (2.5 ml) chopped fresh thyme leaves, plus 6 small sprigs
12 black olives, pitted
1/4 cup (25 g) chopped fresh basil
2 tbsp (12 g) fresh parsley, chopped
Salt and pepper, to taste

In a bowl, mix flour, salt, pepper, and half of the Herbes de Provence.

Wash and pat the conger eel slice dry.

In a large skillet, heat 2 tablespoons of olive oil on medium low heat. When the oil is hot, flour the fish slices all around, tap the excess flour off, and place in the pan. Pan fry the fish for about 3 minutes on each side or until golden brown. Remove and place on a couple of plates. Discard the oil in the skillet then add the last tablespoon of olive oil. Return to the heat.

Sauté onion, garlic, and remaining Provencal herbs in olive oil for 1 to 2 minutes or until onion is soft. Add wine, tomatoes, cayenne pepper, bay leaf, thyme, and olives to the mixture and bring to a boil then reduce the heat and simmer for 15 minutes. Baste with the juices regularly.

122

Return the fish to the pan, cover, and simmer for about 20 minutes. Taste and rectify the sauce seasoning accordingly to your taste.

Just before serving, add basil and parsley and cook for 1 minute. Serve hot as an appetizer or with rice as a main course.

Note: Herbes de Provence are a mix of dry basil, fennel seed, lavender, marjoram, rosemary, sage, summer savory, and thyme.

Fareham Fish and Chips

True British fish and chips are traditionally deep fried in beef drippings that yield a much more interesting flavor to the dish. However, peanut or canola oil works well too.

Estimated time to complete: 1 hour, 10 minutes   Serves: 4

Beef drippings for deep frying, or peanut/canola oil
4 x 5 oz (140 g) thick cod or halibut fillets
8 oz (280 g) self-rising flour, plus extra for dusting
Salt and freshly ground black pepper
10 fl oz (300 ml) cold beer lager
6 large Russet potatoes
Sea salt, to season
1 lemon, cut into wedges
Malt vinegar
1/4 cup (60 ml) tartar sauce

Preheat the oven to 275°F/125°C and the deep fryer to 350°F/175°C.

Peel the potatoes and cut into whatever size you prefer. Wash well in cold water, drain, and pat very dry with a kitchen towel.

Fry potatoes at 350°F/175°C for about 7 minutes. At this point, the potatoes should be cooked but not browned. A potato pressed with the back of a spoon on a plate should crush. This first frying can be done several hours ahead of time.

Sift the flour and a pinch of salt into a large bowl and whisk in the beer to create a thick batter, adding a little extra beer if it seems too thick. It should be the consistency of very thick double cream and should coat the back of a wooden spoon. Season with salt and pepper.

Dust the fish with flour; this enables the batter to stick to the fish. Thickly coat 2 of the fillets with the batter. Carefully place in the hot fat and cook for 8-10 minutes until golden brown and crispy. Remove from the deep fryer, drain, and place on a baking sheet lined with absorbent paper. Keep the prepared fish warm in the oven while you cook the remaining 2 fillets the same way.

124

Once the fish is cooked, raise your deep fryer to 390°F/185°C. When hot, fry the potatoes again for 1 to 2 minutes until golden brown. Sprinkle with salt before serving with the crispy fish. Serve hot with lemon wedges, malt vinegar, and tartar sauce on the side.

Grilled Sea Bream Au Naturel

Au Naturel means cooked plainly without other fancy ingredients. I believe this is the best way to pay homage to this generous bounty from the sea. Salt, pepper, lemon and a great olive oil are plenty!

Estimated time to complete: 30 minutes   Serves: 2

1 sea bream, whole, cleaned and fins trimmed off, head and tail left on
Salt and freshly ground black pepper, to taste
2 tbsp (30 ml) extra virgin olive oil
1 lemon, cut into wedges, for serving
Preheat oven to 400°F /200°C and grill to medium-high.

Rinse the fish inside and out under cold running water then drain and blot dry with paper towels. Season the fish, inside and out, with salt and pepper. Brush with olive oil and grill the fish, turning at a 90° angle with a spatula to make a cross mark grilling pattern. Grill until tender and nicely browned, about 2 minutes per side.

Arrange the grilled fish on a roasting pan. Brush with olive oil and bake in preheated oven for about 10 minutes or until the fish is cooked through to the bone.

When cooked, serve the fish whole with lemon wedges.

Aunt Jeannette's Fig Jam

This is a delicious jam to make with fresh figs. My aunt used figs from a very old tree that was outside her kitchen in Momas. The tree was abundant with fruits that had dark skin and sweet purple flesh. In the fall, when we cooked chestnuts, we would add extra flavor by dropping some fig leaves from the tree into the pot.

Estimated time to complete: 2 hours   Makes: 4 half-pint jars.

3 lbs (1.3 kg) fresh figs, washed, stems removed
2 cups (500 g) granulated sugar
Juice and finely grated zest of 1 lemon

Using a large saucepan, combine the figs, sugar, lemon juice, and lemon zest. Bring to a simmer over medium low heat, stirring constantly. Cover and simmer over low heat for 1 hour, stirring occasionally. Remove cover and continue simmering, stirring frequently, until the mixture thickens. When the mixture gets quite thick, be sure to stir constantly to keep from scorching.

While the figs are cooking, sterilize the jars and lids. Put the glass jars in a boiling water canner about half-filled with water. Bring to a boil. Reduce heat and keep jars in the water.

Put water in a saucepan and bring to a simmer. Reduce heat to low and add the jar lids. Keep in the hot water until ready to use. Do not boil.

Fill the jars with the hot fig jam mixture, leaving 1/2 an inch of headspace. Use a large jam funnel to fill the jars. Wipe jar rims and sides with a wet paper towel. Place lids on jars using tongs, then screw on the rings. Place on a rack in the hot water in the canner. Lower into the water and add enough hot or boiling water to bring the water level to 1 to 2 inches above the jars. Boil jars for 10 minutes. Remove jars from the canner and let cool. Store the jam in the pantry until you wish to serve it. This frees up valuable refrigerator space.

Auntie Jeannette's Sablés

I am so fond of these sablés, just thinking about them makes me smile. My aunt would bring them from the kitchen as if she were carrying a treasure. Often, these shortbread-style cookies were kept in a tin box to protect them from the humidity. They are the perfect compliment to a cup of tea.

Estimated time to complete: 55 minutes   Makes: 2 dozen

9 oz (255 g) all-purpose flour
5.5 oz (155 g) salted butter
2.6 oz (70 g) sugar
1 egg
1 tsp (5 ml) pure vanilla extract
1 egg yolk

Preheat oven to 400°F / 200°C.

In a big glass bowl, soften the butter in the microwave or leave it at room temperature for a few hours. With an electric mixer, blend the sugar and butter. Add the whisked egg and vanilla. Add the flour, mixing it carefully without force until you get an even rounded mass.

Put the mixture in the refrigerator for 30 minutes. Remove from fridge. Flatten the dough down to 1/3 inch (1 centimeter) with a rolling pin (reasonably thick) and cut out the sablés using a pastry cutter.

Place the sablés on a baking tray covered with parchment paper. With a brush, apply the glaze (1 egg yolk whisked with 1 tablespoon of cold water) and sprinkle each sablé with a pinch of sugar.

Bake in the oven for 10 to 15 minutes, depending on the thickness of the biscuits. Remove when lightly golden on top. Cool before serving.

Monsieur Méchain's Pastis Béarnais

Baking is a craft passed down from father to son through many generations of the Méchain family. During my childhood, the bakers expanded their audience by driving a large van throughout the city and countryside, all the way to Momas where my Aunt Jeannette bought their bread and pastis for special occasions.

Estimated time to complete: 2 hours, 30 minutes   Serves: 8

1/2 lb (250 g) all-purpose flour
0.2 lb (100 g) sugar
1 tbsp (15 ml) orange blossom water
0.2 lb (100 g) milk
2 eggs
2 oz. (60 g) butter
0.7 oz (20 g) fresh yeast or 0.3 oz (10 g) dry yeast
1 tbsp (15 ml) anise liqueur (Ricard or Pernod)

Preheat oven to 375°F / 190°C.

In a small bowl, mix yeast in warm, but not hot, milk. Melt butter in a small pan. In a large bowl, sift the flour and mix in the sugar. Make a well in the center of the flour mixture and slowly pour in the milk and melted butter. Mix vigorously to incorporate all ingredients.

Add eggs, one at a time, and then add orange blossom water and anise alcohol. Work the dough until smooth and even. Do this in a bowl as it might be sticky. Transfer everything into a greased tube cake pan, filling the mold half way.

Put dough in a warm place for an hour, or until it rises to about 1 inch from the edge. Bake in preheated oven for 25 to 30 minutes or until a toothpick inserted into the middle of the cake comes out dry. Remove cake from the pan and place on a rack to cool.

Mamie Augusta's Crepes with Sugar

Crepes are French pancakes, thin, light, and made with flour and egg batter. They are often spread with jam, stuffed with fruit, and topped with whipped cream. However, the traditional way of serving them is to simply sprinkle them with sugar. And remember Mamie's advice: listen to the dough!

Estimated time to complete: 35 minutes   Makes: About 20 crepes

1 cup (125 g) sifted all-purpose flour
2 tbsp (30 ml) sugar
1/8 tsp salt = 1 big pinch
1 cup (250 ml) milk
1/2 cup (120 ml) cold water
2 eggs
2 tsp (10 ml) vanilla extract
1/2 oz. (15 g) melted butter
2 crepe pans (10 inches in diameter)
2 tbsp (30 ml) rock salt
1/2 of a baby potato, washed
1 oz. (30 g) butter, melted

In a bowl, mix the sieved flour, sugar, and pinch of salt and make a well in the middle.

In a separate bowl, beat the eggs and whisk in the milk. Mix in by gradually pouring the liquid into the well of the dry mixture. Whisk in a spiral motion from the inside to the outside. Continue until the batter is smooth and no lumps remain. Add the water and vanilla. Check the consistency of the batter. It shouldn't be too runny or too thick. If it is lumpy, pass it through a strainer or blend it with a hand blender. Add the melted butter to the batter. It doesn't require any time to stand.

To clean the pan, add the rock salt and heat for 3 minutes on medium heat then rub the bottom of the pans with a paper towel or rag and discard the salt. Melt the butter in a bowl. Take the hot pan off the heat. Stab the potato with a fork, dip in melted butter, then use the potato to butter the pan; this will avoid burning the pan.

Pour about 1/4 cup (60 millilitres) of batter into the hot pan and tilt it using a circular motion to coat the bottom evenly. Return the pan on the burner on medium-low heat. After 1 to 2 minutes, lift the edge of the crepe with a spatula to see if it is browning. When the underside has begun to brown, flip the crepe over and cook the other side until it is also brown, about 1 minute. Place the crepe on a plate and sprinkle it with sugar.

Repeat the process until there is no more batter left. Yum!

Note: You can enjoy these crepes with sugar or a filling of your choice such as Nutella, honey, jam, etc. If you want to serve crepes as an entree, do not add sugar to the batter.

Note: It is easier to make crepes using non stick pans. I recommend the heavy De Buyer branded steel pans used by most chefs in France.

Madame Crouzier's Pain-Perdus

Our friends, the Crouziers, lived close to us in the Ousse des Bois area; our buildings were separated by a soccer field. Often when I visited their son Dominic in the afternoon, I would find Madame Crouzier making this wonderful recipe. Pain Perdu means "lost bread". This recipe was and still is a scrumptious way to make good use of stale loaves of bread that would otherwise be thrown out - a perfect afternoon snack or meal for hungry teenagers!

Estimated time to complete: 25 minutes   Makes: 6

2 eggs
1/2 cup (120 ml) milk
Pinch of salt
1 tbsp (15 ml) sugar
2 tsp (10 ml) pure vanilla extract
1/2 tsp (2.5 ml) cinnamon
6 thick slices of day old French bread (staler bread is fine as long as you can slice it)
3 tbsp (45 ml) butter
1 tbsp (15 ml) vegetable oil
2 tbsp (30 ml) icing sugar

This simple milk and egg custard is the secret to a great pain perdu recipe. In a large mixing bowl, whisk together the eggs, milk, salt, sugar, vanilla, and cinnamon.

Slice the bread into thick 3/4 inch slices and add to the egg mixture. Toss the slices until all the mixture has been absorbed into the bread. Depending on how stale the bread is, this may take from 5 to 10 minutes. The secret to this recipe is to completely saturate the bread. This is why stale bread is best since fresh bread would fall apart.

In a large non-stick skillet over medium heat, cook the slices in the butter and oil for about 3 to 4 minutes per side until uniformly brown. Be sure the bread slices don't stick to the bottom of the pan.

Serve on a platter with powdered sugar sprinkled over top or with maple syrup on the side.

Gâteau au Yaourt with
Lemon Cream Cheese Icing

This simple cake is one of the first that French children learn to make and is thus a nostalgic favourite of many French chefs. The use of a yogurt pot/cup as a measuring unit adds to the recipe's charm and the lemon cream cheese icing gives it an extra gourmet flair that is sure to please guests both young and old.

Estimated time to complete: 1 hour   Serves: 4

1/2 cup (120 ml) natural yogurt
2 oz. (50 g) salted butter, soft
1/4 vanilla bean, scraped
1/2 cup (100 g) sugar
2 small eggs
3/4 cup (105 g) all-purpose flour
1/2 tsp (2.5 ml) baking powder
1/4 cup (40 g) icing sugar
4-oz. (115 g) cream cheese, room temperature
2 tsp (10 ml) fresh lemon juice
1 tsp (5 ml) finely grated lemon peel
2 tbsp (30 ml) whipping cream

Preheat oven to 350°F / 175°C with rack in middle.

To start the cake, butter a small round cake pan then line bottom with buttered parchment paper. Dust with flour, knocking out excess. Sift together cake flour and baking powder.

In a medium size bowl, beat together soft butter, sugar, and vanilla with an electric mixer at high speed until pale and fluffy, 3 to 5 minutes. Beat in eggs, 1 at a time, at medium speed. At low speed, mix in flour mixture in 3 batches, alternating with yogurt, beginning and ending with flour mixture, mixing until just combined. Spread batter evenly in pan and rap pan on counter several times to eliminate air bubbles.

Bake until cake pulls away from sides of pan and a wooden pick inserted in center comes out clean, 35 to 45 minutes. Cool in pan 10 minutes and then run a knife around edge. Invert onto a rack and discard parchment. Cool completely, about 40 minutes.

For the icing, blend icing sugar, cream cheese, lemon juice, and lemon peel in a bowl. Mix in enough cream to form a thick but pourable icing. Spread over cool cake and allow to set for a few minutes before cutting.

133

Traditional Madeleines

A Madeleine is a traditional small cake from France. Madeleines are identified by their decorative shell-like shape, which they acquire from being baked in special shell-shaped pans. Their flavor is similar to but somewhat lighter than pound cake, with a pronounced butter and lemon taste.

Estimated time to complete: 50 minutes   Makes: 24 pieces

2 eggs
3/4 cup (120 g) of icing sugar
Zest and juice of 1 lemon, strained
1 tsp (5 ml) baking powder
1 cup and 1 tbsp (140 g) of sifted all-purpose flour
3 oz (85 g) melted butter, cooled
Icing sugar to sprinkle

Preheat oven to 375°F / 190°C. Grease two 12-mold Madeleine cake pans.

In the bowl, whisk eggs and sugar vigorously for 3 to 5 minutes or until pale yellow and fluffy. Then, gently mix in the zest and lemon juice. Combine baking powder and flour. Slowly add the dry ingredients and melted butter to the egg mixture in 4 or 5 stages. Let stand for at least 30 minutes in the fridge. Pour the mixture into the Madeleine cake pans.

Bake for 12 to 15 minutes. Turn the pans from time to time to cook evenly. Check if the Madeleine is cooked by inserting a toothpick into the center. It should come out clean.

Remove Madeleines from the molds immediately after cooking. Turn onto a wire rack to cool and set aside. When cool, sprinkle with icing sugar and serve.

Mr. Marcel's Chichis

Mr. Marcel had a rectangular professional deep fryer that allowed him to make long straight chichis. At home you may use a regular deep fryer and shape them into a spiral.

Estimated time to complete: 50 minutes   Makes: 8 chichis

5 cups (1.2 l) of vegetable oil for frying
1 x 1 inch wide strip orange or lemon peel
2 1/2 cups (590 ml) water
1/4 tsp (a pinch) salt
2 tsp (10 ml) olive oil
2 cups (250 g) all-purpose flour
Granulated sugar for sprinkling

Special equipment: A piping bag fitted with a 1inch star opening and a pair of scissors

In a large heavy saucepan, bring water with salt to a boil while covered. Add the olive oil and remove from heat. Immediately add flour and stir vigorously with a wooden spoon until flour and water are well combined (mixture will be stiff and not very smooth). Fill piping bag with some hot dough and wrap a kitchen towel around it to protect your hands.

Heat 1 inch of oil in a 4 quart Dutch oven or a wide 4 inch deep heavy pot over high heat until a deep-fat thermometer registers 375°F / 190°C (oil will be just beginning to smoke). Drop in citrus peel (oil will bubble vigorously) and leave in oil until browned, about 1 minute. Remove the rind with tongs.

Holding opening about 2 inches above oil, squeeze dough into oil in a continuous stream, making a spiral shape. Spirals take practice; have a helper coax dough into a spiral in oil with scissors, keeping dough away from the side of the pot. Stop when dough stream breaks naturally or pot is full.

Note: BE CAREFUL - OIL SPLATTER MIGHT OCCUR.

Cook until underside is golden, about 1 to 2 minutes, and turn over with slotted spoon. Then cook until golden, about 1 1/2 minutes more. Using a skimmer, transfer chichis to paper towels to drain then sprinkle with sugar. Make more chichis in same manner, returning oil to 375°F / 190°C between batches.

Break chichis into pieces if desired and serve immediately, sprinkled with cinnamon powder or with a chocolate dipping sauce.

Apricot Tart with Almonds, Pistachio and Rosemary Frangipane

Frangipane is a classic pastry filling with ground almonds. Here, pistachios are also added. Both the pastry and the filling can be prepared one day in advance.

Estimated time to complete: 1 hour, 45 minutes   Serves: 8

1 1/2 (190 g) cups all-purpose flour
11 tbsp (145 g) sugar, divided
1/4 tsp (pinch) salt
1 cup or 2 sticks chilled butter (230 g), cut into 1/2-inch cubes, divided
10 tbsp (150 ml) chilled whipping cream, divided
2 eggs and 1 egg yolk, divided
1/2 cup (50 g) shelled natural unsalted pistachios
1/2 cup (70 g) slivered almonds
1 tbsp (10 g) fresh rosemary leaves, chopped
1 tsp (5 ml) vanilla extract
1/2 tsp (2.5 ml) almond extract
9 large apricots, halved, pitted
1/4 cup (60 ml) apricot jam
Chopped pistachios
Few rosemary sprigs

Preheat oven to 375°F / 190°C with rack in middle.

To make the dough, combine flour, 3 tablespoons sugar, and salt in processor and blend for 5 seconds. Add 1/2 cup butter and cut using on/off turns until mixture resembles coarse meal. Add 2 tablespoons cream and the egg yolk. Using on/off turns, blend until moist clumps form. Gather dough into ball. Press over bottom and up sides of 10-inch-diameter tart pan with removable bottom. Pierce crust all over with fork. Cover and refrigerate at least 1 hour and up to 1 day.

To make the cream, combine pistachios, almonds, and remaining 1/2 cup sugar in processor. Blend until nuts are finely ground. Add remaining 1/2 cup butter and chopped rosemary and blend to paste consistency. Using on/off turns, mix in the 2 whole eggs, both extracts, and remaining cream. Let stand at room temperature for a maximum of 1/2 hour before using or keep chilled.

Place a layer of foil over the dough and fill with dried beans or rice. Bake 20 minutes or until dough starts to cook, but still lacks color. Remove foil and weights, and spread filling evenly in the crust. Arrange apricot halves, cut side down, close together in concentric circles as top filling, fitting in as many as possible. Bake tart until filling is lightly browned and apricots are tender, about 55 minutes. Cool tart completely on rack.

For the glaze, combine jam and 2 teaspoons water in heavy small saucepan. Simmer over medium-low heat 1 minute, stirring constantly. Strain glaze into small bowl. Push up pan bottom to release tart. Place tart on platter. Brush glaze over tart. Sprinkle chopped pistachios around edge of tart, and decorate with rosemary sprigs.

Strawberry Tartlets with Basil Chiboust Cream

Chiboust—it's not just for Gâteau Saint-Honoré anymore! This rich custard cream preparation gets a modern makeover when infused with basil and paired with sumptuous fresh strawberry tartlets to form a truly decadent summer dessert offering.

Estimated time to complete: 1 hour, 40 minutes   Makes: 10 tartlets

2 cups + 2 tbsp (275 g) all-purpose flour, divided
3.75 oz (3/4 stick) (105 g) cold unsalted butter, diced
7 tbsp (85 g) sugar, divided
1/8 tsp (pinch) salt
1 cup (240 ml) milk
1/4 tsp (a few drops) pure vanilla bean caviar
3 large egg yolks
1 tsp (4 g) icing sugar
1/2 cup (60 ml) heavy cream, whipped
2 tbsp (15 g) chopped basil
4 cups (1 l) whole strawberries, hulled but sliced at the last minute
1/4 cup (60 ml) apricot jam
2 tbsp (15 g) shelled pistachios, chopped

Preheat oven to 400°F / 200°C.

Make the dough in the bowl of a food processor. Blend together the 2 cups flour, diced butter, 1/4 cup sugar, and salt. While the machine is running, add iced water, a few drops at a time, until the dough forms a ball around the blade. Remove from machine, knead briefly, wrap, and refrigerate for at least 20 minutes.

Meanwhile, make the basil chiboust cream. In a clean chilled bowl, whip the cream to soft peaks and reserve in the refrigerator.

In a medium, heavy saucepan, combine the milk and vanilla. Bring to a gentle boil over medium heat. In a medium bowl, whisk together the egg yolks and 3 tablespoons regular sugar, until pale yellow, then whisk in 2 tablespoons sifted flour. Slowly add the boiling milk to the egg yolks mixture, whisking constantly until smooth. Wash the milk pan and return the custard to the clean pan. Return to medium heat and cook, whisking constantly until the mixture thickens

138

and boils for a minute. Never stop whisking or the pastry cream may burn.

Remove from heat and transfer to a clean bowl. Sprinkle some icing sugar on top to prevent formation of a skin that will produce lumps when cold. Cover with plastic wrap, pressing down against the surface. Refrigerate until well chilled, about 1 hour, then before using, fold in the whipped cream and the chopped basil.

To make the tartlets, remove pastry from the fridge and roll it out on a well-floured surface until it is around 0.15 inches or 0.4 millimetres thick. Lightly butter ten 10 x 3 inch tart tins. Line the tart tins with the pastry. Cover the dough with foil and add some baking beans or other weight. The beans create pressure on the dough so that it bakes without puffing up. This step ensures a crisp crust. Be sure to let the crust cool completely before adding the pastry cream and strawberries. The North American culinary term for this technique is baking blind. The French say, cuire à blanc.

Blind bake the pastry in preheated oven for 12-15 minutes until they are firm and golden. Remove the pastry from the oven and allow it to cool. Remove foil and weights.

Fill the tartlet shells with a 1/2 centimeter of basil pastry cream. Wash and hull the strawberries. Slice and garnish the tarts so that the cream is completely covered. In a small saucepan, whisk together the apricot jam and water and bring to a boil. Cook on medium heat, mixing well, and then brush this mixture over the berries. Garnish with some chopped pistachios.

French Quatre Quarts Cake

This is a traditional French cake. Every family has made it since it's so quick and easy. The secret is to weigh the eggs and then use the same weight of flour, butter, and sugar.

Estimated time to complete: 1 hour, 5 minutes   Serves: 4

2 eggs
Flour = same weight as the eggs
Sugar = same weight as the eggs
Butter = same weight as the eggs
1 tsp (5ml) baking powder
1/4 tsp (pinch) salt
1 tsp (5 ml) orange blossom water
1 tsp (5 ml) butter

Preheat oven to 425°F / 220°C with rack just below the middle.

In a large bowl, mix together flour, sugar, slightly melted butter, baking powder, salt, and orange blossom water until dough becomes smooth and homogenized.

Evenly grease a 6 inch round non-stick cake pan with 1 teaspoon of butter. Cut a sheet of parchment paper the same size as the bottom of the cake pan and then place in the pan.

Pour the cake mix into the cake pan and cook for 45 minutes. The cake is cooked when an inserted toothpick comes out dry. Remove cake from the pan while it is still hot.

Let cool completely before serving with your favorite tea.
Note: You may substitute orange blossom water with rum, vanilla, or the zest of any citrus.

CPSIA information can be obtained at www.ICGtesting.com
Printed in the USA
LVOW13s2014240714

395882LV00034B/1157/P